THE
SLENDERMAN
MYSTERIES

THE

SLENDERMAN

MYSTERIES

AN INTERNET URBAN LEGEND
COMES TO LIFE

NICK REDFERN

ISBN: 978-1-63265-112-9
Library of Congress Cataloging-in-Publication Data
available upon request

Cover design by Howard Grossman/12E Design
Forest image by photocosma/depositphotos
Interior by Gina Schenck
Typeset in Minion Pro and Nollanaama

Printed in Canada
MAR

10 9 8 7 6 5 4 3 2 1

"When, lo, as they reached the mountain-side,
A wondrous portal opened wide,
As if a cavern was suddenly hollowed;
And the Piper advanced and the children followed,
And when all were in to the very last,
The door in the mountain-side shut fast."

—Robert Browning,
The Pied Piper of Hamelin: A Child's Story, 1842

ACKNOWLEDGMENTS

would like to give my sincere thanks to all of the following people, without whom this book would not exist: my good friend and tireless literary agent, Lisa Hagan, for all of her hard and dedicated work; everyone at Career Press, including Michael Pye, Laurie Kelly-Pye, Jeff Piasky, Lauren Manoy, Gina Schenck, and Adam Schwartz; Allison Jornlin, for sharing with me her insights into aspects of the Slenderman phenomenon; Tea Krulos, for a thought-provoking and revealing interview; Robin Swope, who went beyond the call of duty in terms of giving me his views on the Slenderman; Ian Vincent, for nailing the connections between the Slenderman and the field of Chaos Magic; Jenny and Loren Coleman, whose work in the field of the Slenderman has proved to be invaluable; David Weatherly, for kindly sharing with me several cases from his files; Mike Huberty, who demonstrated to me that Waukesha, Wisconsin, is a place filled with paranormal activity; close friend Kimberly Rackley, who generously agreed to be interviewed on the issue of her personal encounters; Olav Phliips, of *Paranoia Magazine*, for an eye-opening insight into the Slenderman phenomenon; and, finally, my good mate Simon Wyatt for his phenomenal artwork of the Internet's most infamous monster.

CONTENTS

INTRODUCTION

Imagine the scene: It's the dead of night and you are fast asleep. Suddenly, things change radically and you find yourself *far* from asleep; you are now wide awake but unable to move. You are completely paralyzed. You try to cry out but it's no use. Your heart pounds and your head spins chaotically. Worse still, you see hunched over in the shadows of the bedroom an eight-to-nine-foot-tall skinny and emaciated creature. It is dressed in an old-style black suit, and has a pale face that lacks eyes, a nose, ears, and a mouth. As for its arms and legs, they are almost like those of a spider: long, thin, and spindly. Rubbery, octopus-like tentacles protrude from its torso; they wave and flicker ominously in your direction. To your horror, the night-fiend slowly moves toward you and leans over. Its foul breath makes you wretch. It whispers that you are about to die or that it is coming to take your soul. Maybe you will be its eternal slave in its forested, ancient abode. Now in a state of complete terror, you finally manage to cry out and wake up in a cold sweat. The terrible thing is suddenly gone. You have just had a trauma- and fear-filled encounter with the Slenderman. But, mark my word, he will be back. He *always* comes back eventually.

The Slenderman has curious origins. He began "life" purely as an Internet creation, specifically the work of a man named Eric Knudsen. In June 2009, Knudsen, via the pseudonym of "Victor Surge," uploaded a couple of doctored photos of the Slenderman to the *Something Awful* website forum. In no time at all, others began writing and posting their very own tales of the Slenderman. Short stories, blogs, novels, online games, chat-rooms, and more soon followed. Then, something menacing and sinister happened: People all across the world began to see the Slenderman. Not just on the Internet, not in novels or in the pages of comic-books, but in their homes. In their bedrooms. In mysterious woods. In dreams that rapidly escalated into full-blown nightmares.

The Slenderman had come to life.

INTRODUCTION

Since 2009, countless numbers of people claim to have seen, and been attacked, plagued, and terrified by this skeletal, pale giant in black. But how could such a thing have happened? Is the creature a *Tulpa*, a Buddhist word that means "thought-form"? When enough people believe in something, the theory goes, that same something can stride out of our darkest imaginations and right into the heart of our own reality. By accepting without question the idea that the Slenderman is more than just a piece of Internet fiction are we also giving him some degree of life? Maybe even independent life? If so, can we extinguish that life? If not, does that mean the Slenderman is here to stay?

Another theory suggests that the Internet is slowly becoming self-aware. Could the online world into which all of us are hooked be the culprit? In September 2012, the *Sydney Morning Herald* published an article titled "A self-aware Internet not so far-fetched" and asked, "Could the internet "wake up"? And if so, what sorts of thoughts would it have? Would it be friend or foe? They are important and integral questions, and particularly so when it comes to the matters of the Slenderman and what it really is (Falk, 2012).

Is the Internet turning against us—in a situation not unlike the vast Skynet system in the *Terminator* movies—and attacking us with digital equivalents of our very own online nightmares? Could those same digital equivalents take a running leap out of the Internet and into our very homes? And, particularly so, the Slenderman?

There is no doubt that the saga of the Slenderman has reached extremely disturbing proportions both on the Net and in our world. In 2014, *Newsweek* reported, "In late May, in the Milwaukee suburb of Waukesha, Wisconsin, two 12-year-old girls allegedly lured a friend into the woods and stabbed her 19 times." The terrible attack was undertaken all in the name of—yes, you guessed it—the Slenderman. It was an affair that shocked the people of Waukesha to their very core and gave the Slenderman the widespread infamy he was surely craving (Jones, 2014).

In a January 24, 2015 article that appeared in the U.K.-based *Birmingham Mail* newspaper (titled "Spooky Slender Men spotted in Cannock"), the editor Mike Lockley wrote that an investigation

> ...has been launched in the Midlands following four sightings of Slender Men—long, stick-thin specters feared around the world…. Slender Men have been a part of global folklore for centuries. They may be known by different names, but their harrowing, elongated appearance remains the same around the world (Lockley, 2015).

More and more people are following, and arguably even worshiping and devoting their lives to, the Slenderman as he becomes ever stronger and more physical in our world. Where did he come from? What does he want from us? What are the many witnesses to the Slenderman telling us? Is there just one creature, or are we looking at multiple

Slender*men*? How can we stop him from terrorizing and torturing us? *Can* we stop him? Or has he become an unstoppable, unbeatable nightmare?

These, and many more, are the questions asked and answered in *The Slenderman Mysteries: An Internet Urban Legend Comes to Life.*

1

"THE BEST, NEW MYTHOLOGICAL CREATURE"

At first glance, the ways and means by which the Slenderman was created appear to be very simple. At *second* glance, however, things are just about anything *but* simple. Indeed, many things in life are so often not what they seem to be. With the Slenderman, though, just about nothing is as it seems. As for the wholly down-to-earth explanation for the Slenderman's "existence," it all began in early June 2009, specifically on the 10th of the month. That was when a man named Eric Knudsen chose to do something that some might view as intriguing, others as ground-breaking, and many—from today's perspective—as downright dangerous. Knudsen molded, nurtured, and duly unveiled what is just about the creepiest and most hostile creature that the Internet has ever seen: the Slenderman.

By his own admission, Knudsen had more than a few inspirations for his creature of choice; some were from the world of horror-fiction, others came from the all too real, and all too dangerous, domain of the supernatural. They included the notorious Men in Black of UFO lore, the Mothman, the collective works of H.P. Lovecraft, sinister Shadow People, Zack Parsons' *That Insidious Beast*, the works of Stephen King, and an eerie character known as the Mad Gasser of Mattoon. (You will learn more about all of these as the book progresses.) The goal, Knudsen explained, was to create "something whose motivations can barely be comprehended and causes general unease and terror in a general population." He certainly achieved his goal and way more (slenderman235, 2011).

It's very clear that a great deal of thought went into how, and under what circumstances, the Slenderman was destined to become the bad-boy, rock-and-roll-star of both the paranormal world and the Internet. Given the nature of the Slenderman and his dark deeds in fiction and, later, in reality (as well as in a hazy combination of both) you might very well be forgiven for assuming that the creation of the creature occurred in the darkened bowels of a creepy, old house. Or, even, in the cellar of something resembling Castle Frankenstein on a dark and thundery night. Not so. Actually, the complete opposite is the case. According to one of Knudsen's colleagues, it was a slow workday afternoon when the Slenderman imagery began to emerge in Knudsen's mind and quickly came to fruition. How profoundly odd and down-to-earth that the definitively *un*earthly Slenderman was born amid an afternoon of boredom in the workplace. In no time at all, the Slenderman—phenomenon, meme, and soon-to-be entity—began to take shape. In fact, said Knudsen, "It was pretty spontaneous" (Ibid.).

By now, there was absolutely no going back.

FROM TWO PHOTOS A LEGEND IS BORN

Using the alias "Victor Surge," and prompted by a competition launched by the folks behind the *Something Awful* website to create images of a supernatural variety, Knudsen set out to do his best. Knudsen secured a pair of black-and-white-photos and digitally altered them. He inserted into the pictures a grim, tall, thin monster in a suit. In a *black* suit. Knudsen then uploaded his pair of carefully and skillfully manipulated images to the forum section of *Something Awful*, which is known for running competitions that revolve around Photoshopped imagery. They were the very first images of what became known as the Slenderman. *Rolling Stone's* Bryn Lovitt said of Knudsen's actions:

"The idea was to see who could use their Photoshop skills to create the best new mythological creature. Activity and praise for Surge's tall, faceless ghoul flourished around the post immediately" (Lovitt, 2016).

As for the two photos, they were similar in the sense that both images showed the tall, thin, black-suited and faceless Slenderman in the midst of groups of children. The creature also sported a number of octopus-like tentacles, which waved in the air and beckoned menacingly, and which was admittedly an undeniably great touch. Thus, the Slenderman's infamously unhealthy and dangerous connections to kids and teenagers was born and unanimously accepted. Where there were children, there was sure to be the Slenderman. In rapid-fire time, there was a new boogeyman in town. The ghoulish thing was like a human stick-insect, but an obscene, malignant, and terrifying one. Knudsen increased the interest in his creation by adding fictional captions to the photos, something that gave them an air of genuineness, albeit that certainly wasn't Knudsen's goal.

It is important to note that there was no deception at work here; this was *not* a case of Knudsen creating a hoax and then trying to pass it off as the real deal. Rather, the aim really was just creating a fearful and entertaining entity for the people who gravitated to *Something Awful*. The first caption, dated 1983, read: "We didn't want to go, we didn't want to kill him, but its persistent silence and outstretched arms horrified and comforted us at the same time." The words were attributed to a "photographer unknown, presumed dead" (Vincent, 2011).

The second photo had a date of 1986 attached to it. The accompanying text read as follows:

> One of two recovered photographs from the Sterling City Library blaze. Notable for being taken the day which fourteen children vanished and for what is referred to as "The Slender Man." Deformities cited as film defects by officials. Fire at library occurred one week later. Actual photograph confiscated as evidence (Peters, 2011).

In this second case, the photographer was a "Mary Thomas, missing since June 13th, 1986" (Ibid.).

THE SLENDERMAN COMES TO LIFE

In terms of how the Slenderman came to be perceived as a real entity—rather than just as a creation for, and paradoxically of, the Internet—it's worth noting that the seeds of this "fact or fiction?" angle were sown immediately. In fact, following Knudsen's uploading of the photos, a commenter at *Something Awful*, using the name of "Slidebite," predicted that it would not be long at all before whole swathes of the paranormal research community would come to embrace the Slenderman as a real entity.

The fascination for the Slenderman grew quickly and dramatically. Driven by Knudsen's initial photos, more and more people created their own Photoshopped pictures and posted them to *Something Awful*. Just five days after the phenomenon began, "Thoreau-Up," who was another *Something Awful* fan, commented that the imagery and descriptions of the Slenderman mirrored a monstrous creature from Germany whose origins dates back centuries. Its name is *Der Grossman*; in English that translates to *the Tall Man*. He was a threat to children and lived in the heart of Germany's Black Forest.

It's important to note that, just like Eric Knudsen, "Thoreau-Up" was not creating a hoax or a fantasy. The story of the Tall Man is indeed a very old one and certainly does parallel certain aspects of the Slenderman phenomenon. You'll be further exposed to this proto-Slenderman later on in the book. A good case can be made that it was the comments of "Slidebite" and "Thoreau-Up" that made at least some of the readers of *Something Awful* think there just might have been something about the Slenderman that went way beyond mere fantasy.

Perhaps echoing what "Thoreau-Up" had to say, the mysterious and one-syllabled "I" commented very soon after: "The Slender Man. He exists because you thought of him." "I" then added: "Now try and not think of him" (Weatherly, 2014).

For so many people who were now hooked into the Slenderman phenomenon, trying to wipe the imagery of the creature from their minds was not an easy thing to do. In fact, just about everyone who regularly checked out *Something Awful* was unable to stop thinking about the Slenderman. The monster was already taking hold of minds and souls, and he hadn't even yet achieved an appreciable degree of reality, which is pretty impressive in a curious and disturbing fashion.

As the days progressed, more and more works of fiction on the Slenderman made their way to *Something Awful*. Many of them had a distinct air of reality to them—in the way they were written, at least—even though they were nothing of the sort. Yet again, though, there was this expanding issue of reality meeting fantasy, which grew and grew, and which still exists to this very day.

By the time mid-June 2009 came around, there was yet another development in the saga. "LeechCode5" suggested that the next step should be the production of a found-footage-type "documentary" on the Slenderman. "LeechCode5" could not know how influential his or her words would very soon become. In terms of the chronology, this brings us to the issue of something that quickly became a YouTube sensation. For Slenderman devotees, it still is.

SLENDERMAN: A YOUTUBE STAR

There is no doubt that the next step in the development of the Slenderman saga occurred only days after Eric Knudsen's phenomenon hit the Net with full force. It's a development that is focused on what is known as *Marble Hornets*: a dark and moody horror-driven series that can be viewed on YouTube and which was the brainchild of Troy Wagner and Joseph DeLage. The central character in the series is Jay—played by Wagner—who is a man on a mission to find the answers to a disturbing question: What has happened to Jay's friend Alex (DeLage), a film-student, who has disappeared under mysterious circumstances? We learn that before Alex went missing, he handed over to Jay the tapes of his film, titled "Marble Hornets," which, Jay quickly comes to realize, contain images of a strange and disturbing entity known as the Operator.

The Operator is, you may not be surprised to learn, a Slenderman-like entity. The Operator then gets his grips into Jay by taunting, torturing, and plaguing him endlessly. From there, we see Jay on a mission to solve the riddle of what happened to Alex and the rest of his team and to uncover the truth behind the mystery of the Operator.

To be sure, it's an enthralling, and addictive show. In fact, such is the incredible fascination for *Marble Hornets*, at the time of writing more than *90 million hits* have been

Beware of the Slenderman. *Simon Wyatt, 2017.*

recorded on YouTube. In April 2015, a movie version of *Marble Hornets*, titled *Always Watching*, was released almost a year after the YouTube series ended, ensuring that interest in the Slenderman/Operator continued at a steady pace. One year later, *The Crooked Man*, a character clearly based on the Slenderman, was released, albeit to very little fanfare. It's a movie that leaves a distinctly bitter taste in the mouth, chiefly because it includes a stabbing incident that was so obviously inspired by the May 31, 2014 knifing of a young girl in Wausheka, Wisconsin (more on that in Chapter 7).

POPULARITY FOR THE MONSTER SOARS

When *Marble Hornets* took off in the spectacular fashion that it surely did, it was clear that something important was taking place. And in the way that boogeyman-like tales develop, it was something new. In barely a handful of days, a bit of fun and a fair degree of Photoshopping had become a veritable phenomenon, one which was expanding at an exponential rate. It's not at all surprising that, as *Marble Hornets* grew and grew, so the stories of the Slenderman became evermore creative and thought-provoking. Conspiracy theories quickly became part of the story, too.

In one such online story, we are exposed to "Optic Nerve." It's a powerful and deeply buried agency of the United States' Intelligence community which, we're told, is fully aware that the Slenderman is real, but whose staff state in their classified files, "There is no way on God's green Earth we will be able to do anything to stop this thing." Yes, it was just a created tale designed to entertain. Yes, it gripped people's imaginations. And it gave the impression that perhaps the Slenderman might be something more than the infernal child of Eric Knudsen. On the matter of what else officialdom might have known about the Slenderman, fictional medical files and police records surfaced, again adding weight to the idea that the Slenderman shouldn't be dismissed so easily. The years that have followed show he has definitely *not* been dismissed (Optic Nerve HQ, 2012).

It may sound unlikely or unbelievable, but in roughly a week the Slenderman went from being a complete nonentity to an Internet superstar. The fast-paced development of the phenomenon continued. It would not be long before the fictional Slenderman had a notable counterpart: a *real* Slenderman. In very little time, claims began to surface of allegedly genuine encounters with something that simply could not exist. *Or, maybe, it could.* But how? Let's take a look. Prepare to see the orderly world of reality turned on its head. *Dis*order and uncertainty were right around the corner, looming large.

There is no doubt that June 10, 2009, is the most important date in the entire history of the Slenderman. That, of course, was the date upon which Eric Knudsen's creation was brought to fruition. November 6, 2009, however, is almost as important. On the night of the 6th, on an episode of the hugely popular paranormally themed talk-show *Coast to Coast AM*, the host, George Noory, took a number of calls from people who claimed to have personally encountered the Slenderman. They all described the Slenderman as looking like Eric Knudsen's monster. In some cases, the witnesses claimed the Slenderman invaded their dreams. Others said they saw the Slenderman in the real world.

It was the *Coast to Coast AM* show that really demonstrated what was going on was the beginning of a radical and sinister shift in the Slenderman phenomenon: What was first fiction was now rapidly becoming something else entirely.

Some might suggest that the people who phoned in to *Coast to Coast AM* were hoaxers. Maybe they were, maybe they weren't. But it doesn't really matter. If enough of the *Coast to Coast AM* audience *believed* what they were hearing, then that collective and combined belief would have gone a significant way toward ensuring that the Tulpa version of the Slenderman would soon be up and running. And guess what? *He was.*

2

"IT TENDS TO FREE ITSELF FROM ITS MAKERS' CONTROL"

ll of the available evidence strongly suggests that the Slenderman took a giant leap from the domain of the Internet and into the real world not long after it surfaced at *Something Awful*. In light of this development, one big and important question needs answering: How on Earth could such an unforeseen and calamitous thing have happened in the first place? The possible answers are several in number, as will soon become apparent. Each and every one of those answers is steeped in menace and horror, which is highly appropriate given that the

Slenderman is an entity for whom menace and horror are veritable calling-cards.

We'll begin with what is perhaps the most intriguing theory of all. It's a theory that suggests we, the human race, are responsible for turning online fiction into fear-filled terror and mayhem of a very real type—albeit, perhaps, completely unknowingly. It's a theory that revolves around thought-forms and Tulpas.

CREATING "LIFE"

The phenomenon of the *Tulpa* has its origins in the ancient teachings of Buddhism and is a Tibetan term that roughly translates into English as "manifestation." It is a highly appropriate piece of terminology for the Slenderman. In essence, it is the process by which the human mind can bring some degree of alternative, physical existence to an entity that is created solely within the depths of the imagination, and from within the dream state, too. In other words, and as incredible as it may sound, each and every one of us may well possess the ability to give "life" to certain "things" that don't exist in the same way that we do. That may very well extend to the Slenderman phenomenon.

As amazing as this may sound, there is a dark and danger-filled downside to creating a Tulpa-style thought-form. All too often they have a disturbing habit of running riot and turning against their creators. They become not just troublesome, but deeply manipulative, highly deceptive, and extremely dangerous. Sometimes even close to deadly. It's a case of being extremely careful of what you wish and yearn for—and definitely so if the Slenderman is your particular Tulpa of choice.

Vice.com states the following: "Tulpas remained the preserve of occultists until 2009, when the subject appeared on the discussion boards of 4chan. A few anonymous members started to experiment with creating Tulpas" (Thompson, 2014).

It's intriguing to note that the 4chan members—who refer to themselves as "Tulpamancers" and who are now a sizeable phenomenon of their very own making—are described as middle-class, young children and teenagers, living in urban environments, and primarily Euro-American in nature. Social awkwardness and anxiety, coupled with crippling loneliness and a sense of not belonging, typify many of the 4chan members, by their own admission. And their numbers are growing outside of 4chan. It's these specific emotional issues that have led so many of the Tulpamancers to create their very own Tulpas, from whom, we are told, they derive deep friendship, a sense of kinship, and a feeling of no longer being alone.

Of particular note, 2009, when the 4chan phenomenon of creating Tulpas began, was also the year in which the Slenderman phenomenon kicked off thanks to Eric Knudsen. On this same path, there is no doubt that most of those who have gravitated toward the Slenderman phenomenon are young children and teenagers. Many of them have displayed extreme emotional states, sometimes dangerously emotional states. The tumultuous events that occurred in the city of Waukesha, Wisconsin, in May 2014 amount to the most tragic and horrific example. As we will see, though, the Waukesha affair was hardly a solitary one. The 2014 saga of a married couple named Jerad and Amanda Miller will soon become part of the story as well.

In light of all this, two important questions need to be asked: Is the massive interest in the Slenderman, as well as the claims that he is seen in the real world, nothing more than hysteria and/or a fascination for the supernatural? Or does the process of intensively focusing and dwelling on the Slenderman phenomenon—by an untold number of young kids, such as the Tulpamancers—cause the Slenderman to come into existence from the depths of the human mind?

To answer those questions, we'll begin with the extremely cautionary experience of a woman named Alexandra David-Neel. Hers is a story that, perhaps more than any other, demonstrates how incredibly easy it can be to focus the human mind on a particular phenomenon of supernatural proportions and then have it duly manifest before you. And, today, that includes the Slenderman.

"MY MIND-CREATURE WAS TENACIOUS OF LIFE"

Born in 1868, Alexandra David-Neel had a rich and fulfilling life; it was a life that lasted just short of 101 years. She was someone for whom just about every day was filled with adventure and excitement. She was a disciple of Buddhism, was strongly drawn to the concept of anarchy, and had a particular affinity with Tibet and its people, much of which is described in her acclaimed 1929 book *Magic and Mystery in Tibet*. It is a fine and entertaining tale of road-trip proportions with a large dose of the supernatural thrown in. It was while in Tibet that David-Neel became acquainted—*deeply* acquainted—with the phenomenon of the Tulpa. Like so many people who came before her and since, however, she found herself in the icy grip of a thought-form that, when primed, activated, and called forth, was determined to keep the priceless life to which it had quickly become accustomed.

David-Neel used her own experiences to demonstrate to her readers the extent to which one creates a Tulpa at one's own eternal peril:

> Once the Tulpa is endowed with enough vitality to be capable of playing the part of a real being, it tends to free itself from its makers' control. This, say Tibetan occultists, happens nearly mechanically,

just as a child when his body is completed and able to live apart, leaves its mother's womb. Sometimes the phantom becomes a rebellious son and one hears of uncanny struggles that have taken place between magicians and their creatures, the former being severely hurt or even killed by the latter (David-Neel, 1958).

You would think all of this knowledge would have dissuaded David-Neel from following the path that so many previously trod and paid the price. But no; she was ready and fired up for the challenge. David-Neel knew *precisely* of what she wrote way back in the 1920s, as well as the inherent dangers. Indeed, on one occasion in Tibet she unwisely chose to create her very own Tulpa. She did so in the form of a rotund, beaming, jollity-filled monk. By the end of the experience, however, there was nothing fun-filled or even chubby about her strange creation. As David-Neel described it, she performed certain procedures and rites— all taught to her by her Buddhist friends in Tibet, and all designed to place her into a state of mind that would make the manifestation of the monk a reality. It was a long and drawn-out procedure, one that lasted not for days or even weeks; it went on for no less than *months*. Dedication was most definitely the order of the day.

Finally, the day came when David-Neel saw her creation in her very own abode, if not exactly in what we would call "the flesh." At first, at least, the monk was a character that could only be seen as a brief, shadowy manifestation of something barely recognizable. As time progressed, however, the monk became more and more physical and substantial. One can see this clearly in David-Neel's writing. She said that he eventually "became a kind of guest, living in my apartment" (Ibid.).

It was shortly after her monk was "born" that David-Neel temporarily left her apartment behind and "started for a tour, with my servants and tents." By now, the creature had a strong presence in David-Neel's environment, to the extent that she no longer needed to focus on the monk to make him appear. The monk would now materialize when and where *he* wanted to appear, regardless of what David-Neel's plans might have been for him. This was not a good sign; the tables were slowly, carefully, and less than subtly being turned. As its time in our world progressed, said David-Neel, so did the monk's progression from a shadowy figure to that of a physical entity. On several occasions, she felt his robe brush softly against her. One time, she even felt his hand grip her shoulder. There was nothing playful about any of this, however, as David-Neel soon came to realize—and to her cost (Ibid.).

As time progressed and as the monk became far less like a fragmentary thought-form and far more like a fully formed person, something ominous happened: The Tulpa began to physically change. Its chubby form altered; it became noticeably slimmer and far more toned and lithe. A fat visage was replaced by sculpted cheekbones of the kind that an up-and-coming Hollywood star would kill for. His original smiling and beaming appearance was soon gone. It was replaced by a sly and knowingly evil face. The creature became "troublesome and bold." Then, there was the most terrifying development of all (if "development" is the correct word to use). David-Neel said that the day finally arrived when her monk-of-the-mind "escaped my control." The monster was now fully free of its moorings (Ibid.).

What had begun for David-Neel as an interesting and alternative experiment concerning the question of what amounts to reality, was now a downright state of emergency. There was only one way to solve the problem, a knowledgeable lama told her, and that was for David-Neel to destroy her creation. Just like the unfortunate doctor in Mary Shelley's classic Gothic novel, *Frankenstein*, David-Neel didn't just come to rue the day she created her supernatural thing. She also found it extremely difficult to end its life. It took close to half a year, David-Neel said, before the manipulative creature was finally dissolved and forever wiped from the face of existence. It was far from an easy task, as David-Neel admitted: "My mind-creature was tenacious of life" (Ibid.).

Very much the same could be said of Eric Knudsen's version of the Slenderman; it is likely relishing its lease on life. And it scarcely needs saying that the Slenderman hardly seems to be the kind of character who would be willing to give up everything that he has now attained: countless numbers of eager followers, the ability to manipulate our minds as he sees fit, the means to create mayhem and death, and a sense of overwhelming power.

A BEDROOM ENCOUNTER OF THE TERRIFYING KIND

Another perfect example of how the mind can create monsters that, when unleashed, look just as real and corporeal as us, is that of a woman named Violet Mary Furth, who was born in Bryn-y-Bia, North Wales, in December 1890. She is far better known within occult circles as Dion Fortune, a woman who, at a young age, immersed herself in the worlds of the supernatural, the work of the renowned neurologist Sigmund Freud, tales of the legendary land of Atlantis (of which she had several extraordinary and graphic visions), and ceremonial magic. She also claimed regular contact with so-called "Ascended Masters," powerful beings who were once human, but after numerous reincarnations, became something far more than human and who dwell in higher dimensions than those of our 3-D world. Fortune also claimed contact with the mysterious and ancient wizard Merlin. She went on to write numerous books, including *Through the Gates of Death*, *Aspects of Occultism*, *Sane Occultism*, and *Psychic Self-Defense*, the latter being undoubtedly her most well-known and influential title.

It was in the pages of this particular book that Fortune told an astonishing story, one which may get to the heart of how and why the Slenderman has successfully achieved a strange form of reality outside of the barriers of the Internet. On the matter of how she succeeded in creating a Tulpa, Fortune said:

> The artificial elemental is constructed by forming a clear-cut image in the imagination of the creature it is intended to create, ensouling it with something of the corresponding aspect of one's own being, and then invoking into it the appropriate natural force. This method can be used for good as well as evil, and "guardian angels" are formed in this way. It is said that dying women, anxious concerning the welfare of their children, frequently form them unconsciously (Fortune, 2011).

"A WELL-MATERIALIZED ECTOPLASMIC FORM"

It was at an unspecified time in late 1928 that Dion Fortune created her very own Tulpa, one that was filled with malevolence, and something which was almost certainly dictated by the fact that, at the very same time in question, Fortune's *own* mind was in a distinctly negative and anger-filled state of flux. On the afternoon of the day in question,

Fortune was lying on her bed, brooding and fuming deeply on how she had "received serious injury from someone who, at considerable cost to myself, I had disinterestedly helped, and I was sorely tempted to retaliate (Ibid.)."

From the way Fortune describes things, it sounds as if—while still on the bed—she did not fall completely to sleep, but was plunged into a distinctly altered state of sleep-meets-wakefulness. It was a state that allowed her to create a mind-monster that leapt out of her dark and swirling imagination with truly incredible speed and ease. In that same altered state, Fortune later recalled, "The ancient Nordic myths rose before me, and I thought of Fenris, the wolf-horror of the North" (Ibid.).

Fenris, a centuries-old Scandinavian supernatural beast, was a wolf of paranormal proportions, one that was perhaps far more a werewolf than it was a regular wolf, at least in terms of its sometimes-humanlike appearance. Within Norse lore, it was said to have been the terrifying offspring of the Nordic gods Loki and Angrboda, and the sibling of the serpent Jormungand and the underworld goddess Hel.

Mere seconds after thinking of Fenris in her state of semi-sleep, the beast put in an appearance. In fact, it materialized right next to her on the bed. The appearance of Fenris coincided immediately with what Fortune described as "a curious drawing-out sensation from my solar plexus." She went on to describe the creature as "a well-materialized ectoplasmic form. It was grey and colorless and had weight" (Ibid.).

That the monstrous wolf had noticeable weight suggests that Tulpas are not mere ethereal specters, but entities that, under certain circumstances, can display a fair degree of physicality. This, you will recall, is something that Alexandra David-Neel reported too. On one occasion, she felt her supernatural monk place its hand on her shoulder.

At the time, Fortune had no real meaningful understanding of the nature or concept of thought-forms and Tulpas; it was only *after* her own experience that she chose to look into the matter at a deep level (and to what became almost an obsessive degree). It's notable, though, that she managed to create such a perfect example of the phenomenon without knowing how she achieved it, which may have a major bearing on why so many people today are seeing the Slenderman, but without fully understanding how and why such a situation could ever exist. People are manifesting the Slenderman, but as Fortune's experiences show, you hardly need to be an expert to cause imagination to become reality.

Looking back on that bedroom encounter (bedrooms hardly being unfamiliar to the Slenderman, it should be said) Fortune recalled: "I knew nothing about the art of making elementals at that time, but had accidentally stumbled upon the right method—the brooding highly charged with emotion, the invocation of the appropriate natural force, and the condition between sleeping and waking in which the etheric double readily extrudes" (Ibid.).

What Dion Fortune achieved with the manifestation of a thought-form-based version of Fenris, and what Alexandra David-Neel described in 1929, has its modern-day equivalent with the many and varied Slenderman encounters that have been reported. There is, after all, nothing new under the sun. It's just the appearance that changes.

PHILIP: THE MAN WHO LIVED...BUT DIDN'T

Moving on to the 1970s, there is the particularly fascinating saga of what has become known as the "The Philip Experiment." It was in September of 1972 that the experiment—actually, multiple experiments of a very controversial nature—began. It was all down to the work of the Canada-based Toronto Society for Psychical Research (TSPR). With help from a learned figure within the field of poltergeist activity, Dr. A.R.G. Owen, the group set about achieving something extraordinary: bringing to life the ghost of a man who had never actually existed. Just like the Slenderman phenomenon, we're talking about calling forth a fictional entity to life, which then appears to take on its own independent existence.

The members of the Toronto Society for Psychical Research chose to give their concocted ghost a name. They settled on Philip Aylesford. The group made him into a rich and powerful man who lived in 17th-century England in spacious Diddington Manor (hence the reason why the whole affair has become known as "The Philip Experiment"). Drawings of Philip were made as a means to give the TSPR someone they could envisage and relate to. It also invigorated things to an astonishing degree, as will soon become clear. As time progressed, so did the story of Philip. The researchers decided to give him a wife, Dorothea. They also gave him a tragic end.

In the wholly fictional story created by the TSPR, Philip fell in love with a local Gipsy girl named Margo. Dorothea, overwhelmed by hate and anger for both Philip and Margo, claimed to possess proof that Margo was nothing less than a practitioner of the black-arts; namely, a full-fledged witch. Philip kept his mouth shut on the matter of the secret affair, fearing that if he spoke out in Margo's defense, his respected position as a powerful local figure would be forever and irreversibly shattered. As for Margo, she was burned alive, which was the typical and horrific treatment dished out by so-called witch-finders in England of centuries long-gone. Philip was soon sent headlong into a state of deep depression—a depression that he never escaped from. He blamed himself for Margo's death and, as a result, hurled himself off one of the higher levels of Diddington Manor, an act that all but guaranteed his sudden, bloody death. The group focused intently and extensively on the soap-opera-style saga as they sought to create a Tulpa-based equivalent of poor, doomed Philip. For a while, nothing happened.

Until, that is, it did.

Things changed to a notable degree when Kenneth J. Barcheldor, who was a practicing psychologist, suggested that instead of visualizing Philip into existence, they should call him forth via the tried and tested method of a séance. Barcheldor's suggestion proved to be far more successful than the group could ever have guessed or anticipated; Philip finally came calling. Not in physical form, but by rapping on tables and by other audible means. Philip's character and history had become fleshed out *by the Tulpa version of Philip.* His 17th-century "life" and career were added to—by Philip himself. Of course, Philip didn't really exist at all, at least not in the way we exist. He was the creation of the Toronto Society for Psychical Research and nothing more. But the intense desire of the members of the TSPR to make Philip real achieved exactly that. In an incredible situation, they had successfully birthed a 17th-century man who never lived, but who, amazingly and weirdly, was now communicating with them. And that same 17th-century man began to converse with his creators more and more.

Perhaps that is what we are doing with the Slenderman—albeit largely subconsciously, rather than deliberately—namely, creating the ultimate Tulpa for the Internet age. And just like every single Tulpa that has ever been created, today's suit-wearing, faceless monster of the Net has no intention of going away anytime soon. *We* may have unwittingly opened the door, but it's the Slenderman who wants that same door to remain firmly open. So far, he is doing a very good job of that, much to our cost.

3

"MAGIC AND FICTION WERE STARTING TO HAVE A CONVERSATION"

When it comes to the thorny issue of theorizing what the Slenderman really is or may be, there are few more learned figures in the subject than Ian Vincent. His writings on the subject include "The Slenderman: Tracing the Birth and Evolution of a Modern Monster," "Killing Slenderman," and "Slenderman: Five Years." Vincent is a long-term student of the occult, a professional combat magician, and an exorcist. How's that for an impressive résumé? He is also someone who has dug deep into the controversial concept of the Slenderman now existing in our world, in the shape and form of a fully functioning Tulpa. But he doesn't end there. Vincent also incorporates into his investigations and theories the issue of what is known as "Chaos Magic." It is something that takes matters to an entirely new, dynamic level and which has significant implications on the Slenderman phenomenon. If you are not aware of what Chaos Magic is, you very soon will be. But, first, a bit of background on what it was that got Vincent caught up in the seemingly never-ending matter of the Slenderman.

On how Vincent became so entranced by the Slenderman phenomenon and mythos, he begins by saying:

I started hearing mutterings about Slendy (as Vincent endearingly and amusingly likes to call the fiendish monster in black) on social media, specifically *Marble Hornets*; a remarkable piece of found-footage horror-fiction. This was when it all began, back in 2009, when I became interested. And the creature it was talking about—Slendy—was just something peculiar. The first few episodes of *Marble Hornets*, when I saw it, they genuinely scared me. That figure, the Operator, was so fascinating. I immediately dived in: I went through the entire *Something Awful* thread; *something* was happening. It was definitely a combination of things: it hit a sweet spot and I think it came in at a particular point in time, on the Internet. Its timing was good. It was the right monster at the right time and for the right audience (Redfern-Vincent, interview, 2017).

He continues and comments on not so much the nature of the Slenderman, but the speed with which the phenomenon developed:

> The thing that really specifically grabbed me and made the story interesting enough for me to write articles on it all is the incredible *rapidity* of it; how it took just 10 days from that first appearance of Knudsen's two photos, to the point where *Marble Hornets* was a thing, and there were Wikipedia entries and blogs. And it was also in that precise 10-day window that people started talking about it as being a Tulpa. When that happened, I thought: Now, you've got very, *very* interesting (Ibid.).

"PUT HIM IN A FOREST AND HE BECOMES A PREDATOR"

Vincent makes an extremely good point about the development of the Slenderman phenomenon: "...Slenderman has slipped across the permeable membrane between fiction and reality—occupying a very old definition of the concept of myth, while simultaneously being a child of the most modern aspects of communication" (Ibid.).

He expands further on this particular issue: "It crosses so many different kinds of weirdness: its status as a guardian of liminality, the idea that it controls all thresholds—like a scarier version of Ganesha, the guardian of the gateway of the abyss" (Ibid.).

On the matter of the Slenderman ties to the Tulpa angle, Vincent says:

> I ended up writing a scholarly paper on the fact that the Western version of the Tulpa has absolutely nothing to do with the actual meaning of the word in Tibet. In the original, the thought-form is just the thing you picture in your head when you are meditating as an offering to the gods, like an apple, as an example. The Tulpa is the visualization of the apple in your mind when you pray; that's all it has ever been. But, it's mutated so much to a point where it's now just this go-to idea of if enough people believe in it, it becomes a thing. And, of course, that tied in with things like the Philip Experiment. So, that's what basically dragged me in; it was that immediate grab and then saturating myself with the lore (Ibid.).

Vincent has other thoughts, too, on this issue of how one visualizes and interprets the Slenderman:

> You can project whatever you want [on the Slenderman]; it's neutral. I mean, there is nothing more neutral than a guy in a black suit. But, that completely faceless aspect of it just makes it that little bit more creepy—and there's the elongated arms, too. Then, there's this juxtaposition of the mundane—a guy in a suit—into an unusual setting. In most of the early stuff—2009, Knudsen, and the early stories—specifically it was forests that he kept appearing in. And, when you have a guy in a suit among the trees, it hits a particular kind of the apophenia we have for having once been a prey species one time in our development. If you see a bunch of stuff out of the corner of your eye that looks like it might be a predator, then you act as though it is a predator, because that's an evolutionary-relative success. You see a guy in a black suit on the street and he's just a guy in a black suit. But, you put him in a forest and he becomes a predator. That image really hits a spot (Ibid.).

All of which brings us to the issue of Chaos Magic and how, in Ian Vincent's opinion, it ties the matter of the Slenderman.

"THE MORE CHAOTIC— THE MORE COMPLETE I AM"

"Chaos magic," says Vincent, "is basically a combination of three things: it's Austin Osman Spare's work, and it's Kenneth Grant's work—who also discovered Spare—and his association with Aleister Crowley and his theories that Lovecraft was actually subconsciously connected with a genuine magical current. And, the last one is Robert Anton Wilson" (Ibid.).

It's important that at this point we take a careful look at the lives and careers of Spare, Grant, and Wilson. We'll begin with Spare. Similar to Vincent, Spare was deeply interested in the occult; and just like Vincent, he too was a full-on practicing occultist. Born in England in 1886, Spare was also a skilled painter and someone with an artistic flair for all things alternative. Indeed, he has since been described as both a proto-surrealist painter and an early pop-artist.

Phil Baker, writing for the *Guardian* newspaper, in an article titled "Austin Osman Spare: Cockney Visionary," states that Spare was, for a while, friendly with Aleister Crowley, "the self-styled Beast 666, before they fell out. Spare's innovative approach to magic was a brilliantly self-educated attempt to manipulate his own unconscious, giving his wishes the demonic power of complexes and neuroses and nurturing them into psychic entities, like the old-style idea of familiar spirits" (Baker, 2011).

George Knowles, who has studied the life and work of Spare to an in-depth degree, provides the following words: "In 1921 Spare published *The Focus of Life*, another book of drawing containing his unique magical commentaries. Here he mentions the word *Chaos* in relation to the normality of chaos as the natural order of things and in the self: 'The more chaotic—the more complete I am,' he says" (Knowles, 2017).

Jaq D. Hawkins, the author of *Understanding Chaos Magic*, says that Chaos Magic can be defined as: "…an area of study that disposes of the need for religion, or prepackaged philosophy and superstition in the use of magic. The Chaos Magician seeks to understand the natural laws behind the workings of magic, and the reasons behind the use of ritual in the performance of a magical working" (Hawkins, 2001).

CHAOTIC DEVELOPMENTS

There is, as you will surely already have deduced by now, a growing amount of cross-pollination in this story. And it only continues. It was in 1947, about nine years prior to his death, when Austin Osman Spare met Kenneth Grant, yet another character without whom Chaos Magic would not be what it is today. After Spare and Grant became acquainted, it wasn't long at all before a good, solid friendship developed; it was a friendship that saw Grant promote Spare's near-surrealist-type art whenever and wherever he could.

Aleister Crowley: The Great Beast. *Wikimedia Commons, 1912.*

Grant, who was born in Essex, England, in 1924, not only established his very own occult-driven body, the Typhonian Ordo Templi Orientis, he was also the secretary of Aleister Crowley, one of the most famous and influential magicians and occultists, and whose following is still ever-growing more than 70 years after his death. Following Crowley's passing in 1947, Grant began to expand on Crowley's Thelemite-based concepts (Thelema being a religion created by Crowley in 1904).

The U.S. Grand Lodge, the governing body of the Ordo Templi Orientis, notes that when it comes to the matter of Thelema, "…it is very difficult to make blanket statements about its nature or (still more so) the natures of its adherents. Even the label 'religion' fits Thelema awkwardly in some contexts—it is in other senses a philosophy and a way of life, while also overlapping with the set of practices and symbols commonly called 'Magick'" ("Thelema," 2016).

Controversy surfaced when Grant, after Crowley's death, took over the position that Crowley had held for so long. The cause of the controversy? Grant began to incorporate into the O.T.O.'s ideology the writings of H.P. Lovecraft, which vexed many, including Karl Germer, who ran the United States–based headquarters of the O.T.O. Grant went on to develop a deep respect for (and a fascination with) Hinduism and expanded his work in the field of sex-magic. Grant died in 2011. Remember: Eric Knudsen *also* incorporated some of Lovecraft's most legendary characters into his Slenderman creation in 2009.

As for poet, writer, and definitive visionary Robert Anton Wilson, his role in Chaos Magic cannot be understated. Born in 1932, he was the author of many highly acclaimed works, including *The Sex Magicians*, *Sex and Drugs: A Journey Beyond Limits*, *Reality Is What You Can Get Away With*, and *Chaos and Beyond*. Phil Hine, in his 2010 book *Condensed Chaos*, provides the reader with the following observations:

> An important influence on the development of Chaos Magick was the writing of Robert Anton Wilson & co, particularly the Discordian Society who revered Eris, the Greek goddess of Chaos. The Discordians pointed out the humor, clowning about and general light-heartedness was conspicuously absent from magic, which had a general tendency to become very "serious and self-important." There was (and to a certain extent remains) a tendency for occultists to think of themselves as an initiated "elite" as opposed to the rest of humanity (Hine, 2010).

All of this brings us back to Ian Vincent. He gets to the heart of what it may have been that brought the Slenderman to a form of life. Or, created another version of it.

"YOU COULD WORK IN DIFFERENT MODELS, DIFFERENT MYTHOLOGIES"

On the matter of Slenderman, Vincent continues:

If you're working in magic, it can become real. In Chaos Magic there are techniques where one can try and summon an entity that you *know* to be fictional, absolutely fictional. People have been working with this kind of stuff since Chaos Magic began. Mostly working with H.P. Lovecraft's ideas and stories. I think that it's definitely something you can work with; I've known magicians who have tried to work with Slendy, to

"It was the right monster at the right time." *Ian "Cat" Vincent, 2017.*

become friends with him. It opens up the possibilities of working with that idea of a Tulpa to generate your own thought-forms. And, because it's a fairly easy concept to get across, particularly if you've been reading up on the Slenderman, it birthed what's called Tulpamancy. I think that what happened is that Slendy gave birth to those instead. It's a great image and had its moment, but it was a precursor rather than an exemplar (Redfern-Vincent, interview, 2017).

On a roll now, Vincent expands further on the matter of Chaos Magic and how it began to significantly expand in the 1970s:

For a long time in magic, definitely up until the middle to late part of the 70s, the idea was that you would work within an existing mythology. If you're working in a Christian mythology, you might try and summon the Devil. Or, you might try and talk to a saint, which, obviously, would have connections to practices in Voodoo, but would be syncretized with the saint figure. And, you'd work with producing the Christian symbolism, but while still connecting with these older African-Caribbean entities (Ibid.).

But, around the 70s, what happened was that partly as a result of Kenneth Grant blurring the line between what could be considered actual occult mythology and what is fiction—which is where Lovecraft's works came in to this—certain people started to play with it and mix it all up. Peter Carroll and Ramsey Dukes: They started to experiment with the idea that firstly you could work in different models, in different mythologies; rather than wholeheartedly believing in one—or even in any (Ibid.).

Carroll is the author of a 1987 book, *Liber Null & Psychonaut*, which is essential reading for anyone wanting to learn Chaos Magic inside and out. As for Dukes, his real name is Lionel Snell and he's someone who has made excellent studies of the life and works of Austin Osman Spare, as is demonstrated in 1972's *Agape Occult Review*. Dukes/Snell is also a skilled magician.

Vincent says:

> So, there's this kind of area where—with Carroll and Dukes—magic and fiction were starting to have a conversation with each other. And, basically, that's the core of Chaos Magic. Chaos Magic is not *always* about working with a fictional entity; that has now kind of split off and become a separate, though overlapping, area of pop-culture magic. So, now, you've got people who are working with the Marvel [Comics] version of Thor, rather than the actual Nordic version of Thor. Separate, different entities, but with some overlap. And occupying different areas. It comes down to that core idea of belief. Something that can be controlled. You can say: "I'm going to choose to believe wholeheartedly in Marvel's *Thor* for six months. Or, until I get a magical event happen which is sufficiently convincing to make it feel like I have contact.
>
> This is an old idea that goes back as far as Crowley, who exalted his students to do this process with

a god-form; you pick a deity and you work with it, and you absolutely obsess yourself with it; you build altars around yourself with the great smells and bells related to that god-figure. You keep working, you keep invoking until you get the god turning up. You have that experience and then you stop. You clear everything away and you start again with a different god. Once you've done that, three or four times, the concept of what gods are, and what belief is, becomes a very malleable thing (Ibid.).

This all sounds like a very plausible explanation for how, under carefully planned and executed circumstances, the Slenderman went from being Eric Knudsen's creation to something very different entirely. The difference, perhaps, was that Knudsen was not aware that he was creating "life," whereas Chaos Magicians are acutely aware of what they are doing—for the most part. I say "for the most part" because of another prime example of the inadvertent creation, and unleashing, of a fictional entity in the real world.

A COMIC BOOK CHARACTER STALKS ITS CREATOR—WHO HAPPENS TO BE A MAGICIAN

There is, as Vincent notes, another "great example" of how Chaos Magic can create a real-world version of a fictional entity. Perhaps it is sometimes done unknowingly, which may also play into the way in which the Slenderman is now its very own entity. That "great example" revolves around a man named Alan Moore and his unsettling encounter with a character named John Constantine. And, I *do* mean a character—a fictional one of nothing less than Moore's very own making (Ibid.).

If you are into comic books, you will know the name Alan Moore. He is the brainchild behind the likes of *V for Vendetta* and *Watchmen* (both of which were made into mega-bucks movies). He also wrote for the popular U.K.-based comic book *2000 A.D.*, first published in 1977 and still going strong. And then there is the fact that Moore is both a ceremonial magician and an occultist, which brings us back to the matter of John Constantine. The creation of Moore, along with John Totleben and Steve Bissette, John Constantine is a kind of anti-hero who was brought to the big-screen in 2005 when Keanu Reeves took on the role in the movie *Constantine*, which raked in a very respectable 230 million dollars.

Ian Vincent tells an extremely strange story about Alan Moore and his fictional creation of John Constantine. Vincent notes that Moore is a "practicing magician," which may have a bearing on how and why his comic book hero came to life, and in much the same way that the Slenderman has. Vincent reveals: "Moore actually saw John Constantine in a café on the South Bank in London [England]. He is a character which Moore had absolutely created himself, but the complete spitting image of John Constantine walked right past him" (Ibid.).

The above is indeed true, as Moore himself has admitted.

The specific location, says Moore, was Westminster, London. As for the encounter, it took place not too long after the John Constantine character had been created by Moore, Bissette, and Totleben for DC Comics. At the time the Constantine manifestation occurred Moore was doing nothing more than munching on a tasty sandwich when something fantastic occurred: John Constantine walked right by an amazed and dumbstruck Moore. And this wasn't just a regular man who vaguely resembled the John Constantine character, who, appearance-wise, was actually based on the singer Sting. He was wearing the very same trench coat that Moore had come up with and his hair was in Constantine's short style. Moore said, "He looked exactly like John Constantine. He looked at me, stared me straight in the eyes, smiled, nodded almost conspiratorially, and then just walked off around the corner to the other part of the snack bar" (McGrath, 2012).

Rooted to his chair, Moore debated on whether he should follow his comic book creation, or if he should just continue to eat his sandwich. Food won. Curiosity did not. For Moore, it was what he termed the "safest" option. He may well have been right. Moore summed things up succinctly: "I'm not making any claims to anything. I'm just saying that it happened" (Ibid.).

Ian Vincent added, "I spoke to Alan about it last year [2016], actually, and he's *still* freaked by that, 30 years later.

It still does his head in. This is a man who works with a god-form which is *known* to be fiction" (Redfern-Vincent, interview, 2017).

Alan Moore was not alone: "jackdirt" says, in "A Chaos Magic Primer," that there was a period of time when he succeeded in calling forth "the persona" of multiple types of famous cartoon characters. He states: "Given a cartoon as the popular idol of the time, it seemed an appropriate avenue to pursue. After all, things only have the power we give them. The success of summoning and interacting with the likes of Bugs Bunny, Roger Rabbit, and Pikachu were nothing short of bizarre."

In a roundabout way, all of the above can be said to go a long way toward explaining how and why people see the Slenderman.

Finally, we come to Ian Vincent's last words on his research into the field of the Slenderman:

> I would say that Slenderman shows us that the things we *know*—the things we *really* know—are the creations of our own imagination and can take on a greater reality than we generally suspect. Or even give allowance for. There are ways, under the right circumstances, for any piece of mythology, or any piece of fiction—comic books, novels, films—to take on a reality far greater than was ever intended. Sometimes, that can bite us. The flavor of the mythology isn't always the governing factor, as to whether it

becomes dangerous. It's entirely situational. There's a timing to it. Sometimes, it'll be just a one-day wonder. Or, it might genuinely implant itself into peoples' minds. But, if it's the right idea, and at the right time, it can become a smash success. Like Slenderman (Redfern-Vincent, interview, 2017).

4

"IS ALL THAT WE SEE OR SEEM BUT A DREAM WITHIN A DREAM?"

I f you think the concept of the Slenderman surfacing in the real world as a mind-created Tulpa or thought-form is strange, there is a very different, but equally controversial and intriguing theory that might help solve the puzzling existence of the Slenderman (or at least a significant part of it). It is a theory that suggests the Internet is responsible for the emergence of the creature. No, we're not talking about publicity on the Net provoking and expanding on the craze for the skinny, suit-wearing monster. What we are talking about is the Internet quite literally unleashing among us a real equivalent of Eric Knudsen's creation. But, you may very well ask, how on Earth could such a thing occur? The answers—like everything else surrounding the Slenderman—are steeped in high-strangeness.

Admittedly, it is a theory that demands we accept something startling as reality: Since its large-scale inception in the 1990s, the Internet has become self-aware—to a certain degree, anyway. It is also a theory that suggests the Internet is now its own intelligent entity, one that is capable of rational thought, having a high degree of consciousness, and even the ability to manipulate us, the human race, all without us realizing what is going on before our very eyes. That may include manipulating us even further by plunging us into real-world equivalents of the simulated domain of *The Matrix*.

Or, have we *always*—and unknowingly—lived in a virtual reality–based world, a highly sophisticated realm that the Slenderman can negotiate with disturbingly skillful ease?

A CREEPY ODYSSEY

The notion of machines, computers, and sophisticated technology effectively enslaving and manipulating us, the human species, is nothing new; it has been a staple and favorite part of the domain of science-fiction writers and fans for decades. Take, for example, Stanley Kubrick's acclaimed 1968 movie *2001: A Space Odyssey*. It is notable that one of the central figures in the film is a computer. Its name is HAL 9000, Hal standing for Heiristically Programmed Algorithmic Computer. Unlike self-aware machines in so many other sci-fi movies, HAL is not presented as a clunking robot or as a rampaging *Terminator*-style cyborg. For the most part all we see of "him" is a red eye. In fact, it's a camera lens, one of a few that pepper the *Discovery One* spaceship, and all of which HAL is hooked into. When we are introduced to HAL, the ship is headed for the planet Jupiter and captained by doctors Frank Poole and David Bowman.

As for how HAL communicates with the crew, it's exactly how we communicate: via a voice. HAL's vocalizations, however, are eerily and constantly calm, whether the circumstances onboard are good, bad, or dangerously fraught. Yet, as the movie progresses we see that HAL's air of calmness is soon replaced by what begins as a degree of rebelliousness and which quickly spirals into full-blown murder. Seeing that HAL is rapidly becoming something not unlike a spoiled, insane, deadly brat, Bowman manages to disconnect HAL. As the memory and character of the crazed computer begin to fragment into nothingness, we see HAL, in the final stages of his existence, rendered into a state of overwhelming fear—the same kind of fear we all have of death and the possibility of an eternal, lights-out oblivion. HAL is, perhaps, the most unsettling example of what could happen if our computer-based technology advances in leaps and bounds and *it* becomes the master and *we* become the slave.

Now, back to the entity that made Arnold Schwarzenegger a star.

FROM SELF-AWARE TO NIGHTMARE

Fans of *The Terminator* movie franchise will recall that one of the key "entities" in the series is Skynet. It is a vast computer network that is designed to keep the United States safe from a nuclear attack. As Skynet becomes more and more powerful and technologically advanced, however, it suddenly becomes self-aware. The unforeseen result is that Skynet interprets *every* human on the planet as a threat, *not* just the Russians or the Chinese. It tries to ensure our extinction, and ensure the rise of the machines by launching an all-out attack on the enemies of the United States, forcing those same nations to quickly retaliate. The outcome is inevitable: global thermonuclear warfare, the end of civilization, and the annihilation of nearly all of humankind.

Then there are *The Matrix* movies. In the phenomenally successful series starring Keanu Reeves, Carrie-Anne Moss, and Laurence Fishburne we are introduced to a world that is identical to the one we all live in, but in "reality" is nothing of the sort. The rise of Artificial Intelligence in the 21st century led the human race to go to war against increasingly powerful machines and computers that had no wish to play second guest to us. Unfortunately, we lost the war and the machines won.

In the movies the human race is kept in check in a very strange and disturbing way: We are no longer born and, instead, we are *grown* in vast and endless factories. The machines, meanwhile, "feed" on our bioelectricity for "fuel." But how do they prevent us from rising up against them? Here's where we get to the crux of the story (and to the crux of the title of the movie franchise, too).

The world we *think* and *assume* we live in is nothing but an infinitely advanced computer-based simulation. It is something akin to a sophisticated dream—albeit a vast online dream, one that we are all unknowingly hooked into. Our real lives, from birth to death, are spent endlessly sleeping in large pods. They are pods in which we are kept alive and fed, ensuring nourishment for the machines. Occasionally, there is a glitch in the Matrix, which can provoke the likes of déjà vu in our unreal environment. Even less occasionally, someone will break free of the chains of the Matrix and fight against their deadly controllers and learn the shocking truth, which is exactly what happens across the course of the trio of *Matrix* movies.

THE MATRIX: NOT JUST A MOVIE?

It is notable that *The Matrix* movies have their own Slenderman-style characters, with a liberal amount of the Men in Black thrown in for good measure. They are referred to as "The Agents," highly sophisticated entities uploaded to the Matrix by their creators. Their job it is to prevent anyone from getting close to the truth of the simulated world of the Matrix. The Agents are the Slenderman-meets-the-MIB: They wear black suits and thin black ties, they are completely lacking in emotion, they can alter time and space, and they can change reality as they see fit.

A *very* similar scenario is presented in a less well-known movie that came out in 1998, one year before *The Matrix* was released. *Dark City* presented a world that is asleep but thinks it is awake. The sun never surfaces and no one thinks to question why. Reality and time are warped and manipulated by creepy, pale-faced things that go by the names of—to offer just a few—Mr. Hand, Mr. Book, and Mr. Rain. The hairless things wear the ubiquitous black hats and black outfits. In fact, so close are the storylines between the two movies, it has led to loud and vocal accusations and suspicions that the makers of *The Matrix* simply jumped on the *Dark City* bandwagon and took sizeable chunks from the latter's script. On this point, consider the following from "Takineko" at the Retro Junk website: "I remember watching *The Matrix* for the first time and thinking to myself, 'I've seen this movie. This is *Dark City* all over again!' The similarities between these films are uncanny. I doubt anyone who's seen both movies would have been oblivious to this" (Takineko, 2017).

In 2004, Rob Lund, at the Electrolund website, wrote: "By now, everyone has either seen or heard of *The Matrix* trilogy. Not as many people have seen *Dark City*, though the two share some striking similarities. Both are stunning achievements in modern science fiction and thematically alike" (Lund, 2004).

"SHOULD WE BE AFRAID OF IT?"

The possibility that the present-day Slenderman is the product of a self-aware Internet, or of a virtual reality world so vast and advanced that we are incapable of seeing through the ruse (most of the time, at least), is an intriguing one. After all, consider this: Bigfoot is a creature said to live in forests, Scotland's Nessies dwell in the deep waters of Loch Ness, sea-serpents inhabit the world's oceans, and the Abominable Snowman (or Yeti) roams the icy Himalayas. The Slenderman, though, is a very different kettle of fish. Unlike all of the strange monsters referenced, the Slenderman is not restricted to, or even tied to, a specific geographical location. Rather, the Slenderman's only ties are to…*the Internet*.

The Slenderman was, in effect, uploaded to the Internet by Eric Knudsen in 2009, as we've seen. Then, according to multiple witnesses, it chose not to remain on the Net for long and, instead, took a mighty leap into the heart of our world. Or, maybe, into our virtual reality—and in much the same way that *The Matrix's* black-suited "Agents" do likewise. Could the Internet be responsible for creating such incredible levels of interest—obsessions, even—in the Slenderman? What do Internet experts make of this theory that the Internet might become the real equivalent of HAL 9000 in *2001: A Space Odyssey*; a crazed, super-powerful entity in its own right? You may be surprised at the number of learned, respectable people who think that could indeed be the case.

Ben Goertzel, who oversees the Artificial General Intelligence Research Institute, states the following: "The Internet behaves a fair bit like a mind. It might already have a degree of consciousness" (Brooks, 2009).

Then, there's Francis Heylighen of Belgium's Free University. He views consciousness as a variety of means by which the processing of data can be made easier and far more efficient. Heylighen says: "Adding consciousness is more a matter of fine-tuning and increasing control than a jump to a wholly different level" (Ibid.).

Professor Francis Crick, a computational neuroscientist at the San Diego, California–based Salk Institute, made an eye-opening observation on this particular topic: "The growth of the Internet over the last several decades more closely resembles biological evolution than engineering" (Sejnowski, 2017).

Robert Sawyer, the author of a trilogy of well-received sci-fi novels on the issue of the Internet becoming self-aware, says that the ever-increasing growth of the Internet will inevitably reach a "tipping point," after which, "you can't do anything about it. Should we be afraid of it? Absolutely" (Falk, 2012).

Has a self-aware Internet created its own version of the Slenderman? There is some evidence this may be the case. Prepare to indulge yourself in a story of eerie proportions, one that just might vindicate the theory that the Internet has begun to manipulate us, to toy with us, and even to send us to the point of irreversible madness.

"WE ARE FRIENDS NOW"

"Lacy" is a trainee flight-attendant from Erie, Pennsylvania. She has had truly bizarre experiences with the Slenderman, although, she certainly wishes that was not the case. Most interesting of all, those experiences began only days after she finished reading Robin Swope's 2012 book *Slenderman: From Fiction to Fact.* Lacy shared her story with a group of attendees, including myself, at the September 2016 Mothman Festival in Point Pleasant, West Virginia. By her own admission, Lacy, like a lot of people, very quickly became overwhelmingly obsessed with the saga of the Slenderman, reading all that she could on the subject. And, as if in response to that growing obsession, the Slenderman paid her a visit of sorts.

It's important to note that Lacy did not see the Slenderman in 3-D, physical form. Rather, she encountered him...*on her laptop.* As Lacy explained, she always keeps her device on a coffee table in her living room. On several occasions beginning in July 2016, while she was watching television late at night, Lacy's laptop, which was in sleep-mode, woke up. But it did more than that. *Way* more. Lacy says that as the laptop exited sleep-mode, there was a very brief image on the screen of what Lacy described as looking like a cross between a man and a long-legged bug, which is admittedly a perfect way of describing the spindly, bony monster that is now so infamous and feared. She pondered for a few moments on the possibility that lights and shadows in the room had caused the freak apparition. But in her heart—which was by now *thumping*—she knew that was not the case. That became even clearer when, two nights later, a similar thing happened again.

On the second occasion, Lacy's laptop once more came to life and the Slenderman came calling again. This time, however, the image on the screen was that of the Slenderman's face. The eyes, the nose, and the ears were all missing, which is what most witnesses to the Slenderman describe. Terrified, Lacy fled her apartment and spent the night at her mother's house. In case you're wondering, no, she didn't take her laptop with her.

The third and final incident occurred around three weeks later, as Lacy sat on the floor of her living room wrapping Christmas presents. She braced herself as her laptop exited its slumber shortly after 11 p.m. A deep but quiet voice uttered a few chilling words: "We are friends."

Then, the laptop returned to its sleep-mode. Enough was enough. Such was the sheer level of Lacy's terror, she completely dropped her research into the Slenderman, deleted all of her files on the subject, and—wait for it—she even *burned* her copy of Pastor Swope's book in a metal container in her mother's yard. Her Slenderman, which gave all the indications of being a creation of the Net, did not return again.

Although she has absolutely no intention of returning to the world of the Slenderman, Lacy solidly believes that her extensive research into the phenomenon caused the Internet to realize what she was doing (as incredible as that may sound) and chose to give her what she wanted, namely an encounter with the Slenderman. For Lacy, it was a case of "be careful of what you wish for," because what you get may not be what you want.

Now, we'll take things to an even stranger level. It is time to address the theory that *The Matrix* may not be so fictional, after all.

THE MOST TERRIFYING ILLUSION OF ALL: THE SLENDERMAN

The idea that reality is not what it appears to be, that we are not in control of our lives, and that we may be living in something akin to an orchestrated, technological dream world, is unsettling. It might not be just an idea. It's possible that this is *exactly* what is going on. Ray Kurzweil, Google's director of engineering, opines: "Maybe our whole universe is a science experiment of some junior high-school student in another universe."

Neil deGrasse Tyson, the director of the American Museum of Natural History's Hayden Planetarium, says of the possibility that we are all living in some form of computer-based program, "I think the likelihood may be very high." He adds: "If that's the case, it is easy for me to imagine that everything in our lives is just a creation of some other entity for their entertainment" (Moskowitz, 2016).

In the summer of 2016, Elon Musk, the CEO of SpaceX, a U.S.-based aerospace manufacturer, publicly stated that, in his opinion, the chances of us living in a "base reality" are "a billion to one" (Solon, 2016).

The BBC notes of Musk's theories: "Musk and other like-minded folk are suggesting that we are entirely simulated beings. We could be nothing more than strings of information manipulated in some gigantic computer, like the characters in a video game" (Ball, 2016).

Perhaps one of those "entirely simulated beings" is the Slenderman, effortlessly inserted into our virtual world. Of course, all of this provokes important questions: If we *are* all living in a Matrix environment, then who created it? The Slenderman? An army of Slender*men*? An entire world of them? How about a veritable *universe* of them? With those uneasy questions in mind, it is perhaps apt to quote a brief

"IS ALL THAT WE SEE OR SEEM BUT A DREAM WITHIN A DREAM?"

extract from Edgar Allan Poe's poem *A Dream Within A Dream*: "Is all that we see or seem but a dream within a dream?" (Poe, 1849).

Still on the matter of quotes, we'll end this chapter with one made by Laurence Fishburne's character Morpheus in *The Matrix*. He says to Neo (played by Keanu Reeves): "Have you ever had a dream, Neo, that you were so sure was real? What if you were unable to wake from that dream? How would you know the difference between the dream world and the real world?" (*The Matrix*, 1999).

5

"FEAR OF THE GAS MAN"

One of the most important factors in the development of the Slenderman mythos—and the subsequent surfacing in the real world of what can only be described as a living equivalent of a fictional creature—is that which concerns Eric Knudsen's inspirations for his now famous creature. As noted in Chapter 1, more than a few of those inspirations were not fictional characters at all. They were real, supernatural entities, including the Mothman of Point Pleasant, West Virginia; the Men in Black; the Shadow People; and an eerie creature known as the Mad Gasser of Mattoon. Even infernal monsters encountered by none other than horror legend H.P. Lovecraft were important parts of the Slenderman's imagery development.

It's notable, and almost certainly not a coincidence, that all of these particular "things" which Knudsen chose to toss into the mix have the ability to invade peoples' dream-states, just like the Slenderman—even H.P. Lovecraft's fictional entities, as we'll shortly see. This eerie blending and meshing of fiction and fact almost certainly had a bearing on the Slenderman's ability to come to life, albeit what amounts to a very strange form of life. It's now time to dig ever further and deeper into the lives of these strange creatures, and the uncanny realms in which they dwell, to see how the uploading of a couple eerie black and white photos has brought us to where we are today. We'll start with the strange saga of the aforementioned H.P. Lovecraft.

The influence of H.P. Lovecraft

Although H.P. Lovecraft is seen by many horror enthusiasts as *the* definitive figure in the world of supernatural fiction, not everyone is quite so sure that Lovecraft's work is wholly fictional in nature. That might sound strange, but bear with me. There is a school of thought that suggests the fantastic worlds, the ancient cities, and the terrible creatures Lovecraft wrote about were unknowingly provoked by glimpses of *real* worlds—supernatural realms accessible to the man while he was deep within the dream state, possibly even while traveling in an astral form (an issue to which we will return in a later chapter). As we have seen, the Slenderman very often invades peoples' lives as they dream, that is, when they are unable to prevent what amounts to a full-blown supernatural assault.

Lovecraft was born in Providence, Rhode Island, in 1890. He was a strange, eccentric, and highly controversial character, and that's putting matters very mildly. He was a racist, someone who found it incredibly difficult to make friends and to socialize, and who was a spectacular failure when it came to getting close to women. His sex life was practically non-existent, and although his writings are currently loved by millions, he spent much of his life living in utter poverty. Malnutrition and cancer took him in 1937 at the tragically young age of just 46. It's a wonder that Lovecraft even lived that long, as dark thoughts of suicide were seldom far from his constantly tortured mind. Although, it's fair to say that they may have been self-indulgent cries for help, rather than real desires on Lovecraft's part to end his life.

There is no doubt that one of Lovecraft's much-revered stories is "The Call of Cthulhu," which was penned in 1926 and appeared in the pages of *Weird Tales* magazine approximately two years later. In the story, Cthulhu—a terrible and vile thing of the deep—is described as "a monster of vaguely anthropoid outline, but with an octopus-like head whose face was a mass of feelers, a scaly, rubbery-looking body, prodigious claws on hind and fore feet, and long, narrow wings behind" (Lovecraft, 2009).

Cthulhu is also said to be what amounts to a human caricature and has multiple tentacles. Does this latter point not strike a chord? It certainly should, as a tentacled, human caricature is a perfect description of the Slenderman, as portrayed by Eric Knudsen. But Lovecraft, despite all of his many flaws, his wholly unforgivable and racist prejudices, and his odd characteristics, was just a gifted writer of horror stories and nothing else. Right? Well…*maybe not*. Here's where we *really* go down the rabbit-hole.

THE INVASION OF THE NIGHT-GAUNTS

Donald Tyson has studied the life and career of H.P. Lovecraft to a very significant degree. He is also the author of a number of acclaimed books on Lovecraft (and Lovecraft-related themes), including *The Dream World of H.P. Lovecraft* and *The 13 Gates of the Necronomicon*. Tyson's combined body of work makes a formidable case for the notable theory that Lovecraft's stories were *not* the collective results of his own swirling mind and imagination. Tyson suggests that Lovecraft's stories were provoked by glimpses of long-forgotten lands and civilizations, terrible beasts, monstrous creatures, and more—some of our world, and many more the products of other universes and multiple dimensions. They were, however, things not seen in our normal reality. Rather, they were encountered in the one distinctly altered state of mind that all of us succumb to each and every night of our lives: the mysterious domain of dreams. Or, in Lovecraft's case, his terrifying nightmares.

It's very notable that as a child, and as he slept, Lovecraft was plagued by fear-filled visits from what he termed the "Night-Gaunts." They appeared, as Tyson noted, in Lovecraft's bedroom and in the form of a "black silhouette." In a 1916 letter written to a friend, Rheinhart Kleiner, Lovecraft said that the Night-Gaunts were "rubbery to the touch." And, as Tyson worded it, appeared as "living shadows." Most notable of all, Tyson reveals, the most terrifying aspect of the Night-Gaunts was "*their complete lack of faces* [author's italics]," a feature that applies to the Slenderman, too. Dozens of Night-Gaunts would descend upon poor, sleeping Lovecraft in the dead of night and would cruelly haul the petrified writer into the dark and cloudy skies high above. They would then drop him from incredible heights, at which point Lovecraft would always awake from the "dream" in a sweat-soaked, cold and clammy, fear-filled fashion. It was a hell of a way to spend the night (Tyson, 2010).

KEEPING IT IN THE FAMILY

Donald Tyson suggests that Lovecraft's Night-Gaunts may have been something more than the products of fantasy and the subconscious. *Much* more. He says: "Lovecraft was more than merely a dreamer. Night after night he engaged in intuitive astral projection." And, there are also these words from Tyson, which are highly revealing:

> At the start of his career as a writer of cosmic horror tales, Lovecraft did little more than set his dreams and nightmares down on the page, and indeed he sometimes wondered if he could even claim credit as the author of the stories, since he was not so much composing them as narrating what he had seen in sleep (Ibid.).

It's also worth noting that Lovecraft's mother Susie Lovecraft had her own encounters with the Night-Gaunts. In Susie's case, however, she saw the monsters when she was *wide awake*. If the creatures were merely the product of H.P. Lovecraft's own mind and nothing else, how on Earth could that be? Well, the answer is very simple: It *couldn't* be. Tyson, however, has an answer for this odd conundrum:

> In sleep, the mind becomes receptive, and there is an inherent receptivity between members of the same family. Susie was already emotionally and mentally unstable. She may well have had the stuff of her son's nightmares impressed on her mind so deeply while she slept, that she began to see shadow creatures of nightmares while she was awake (Ibid.).

So, we have Lovecraft encountering dark, shadowy figures in the dead of night—creatures that were noted for not having faces—and we also have Lovecraft conjuring up images of hideous, rubbery, monsters with tentacles, most famously found in the tales of Cthulhu. They were all supernatural entities that invaded and manipulated Lovecraft's dreams, and to incredible and torturous degrees. Such was the power of these experiences, the creatures even impacted on Lovecraft's own mother. Could they have had an impact on Eric Knudsen, too?

Knudsen may well have been inspired by all of this imagery when he chose to create the Slenderman, as Knudsen has indeed cited Lovecraft when it comes to the creation of the Slenderman. But here's the most important part of all: If the origin of Knudsen's Lovecraft-linked inspiration was supernatural in nature, as it certainly appears to have been for Lovecraft himself, then that may explain how and why Knudsen's Slenderman chose to walk away from the Internet and invade peoples' nightmares and dreams in the real world of the 21st century. From Lovecraft's tales to Knudsen's imagination, there may not be too much difference. It's a definitive case of what goes around comes around.

Now, we'll take a look at another of Knudsen's inspirations for the Slenderman.

MADNESS DESCENDS UPON THE CITY OF MATTOON

It was in the 1940s, when World War II was still raging, that the people of Mattoon, Illinois, found themselves terrorized by a malevolent entity known as the "Mad Gasser of Mattoon." Just like the monsters that constantly tormented H.P. Lovecraft as he slept, the insane gasser, on a number of occasions, turned up while his victims slept. Most of those victims were women, home alone, whose husbands were away fighting in the War, either in Europe against the Nazis or in the Pacific arena against the Japanese.

Matters began when the Raef family had a most unwelcome visitor: The home was quickly overwhelmed by a sickening odor. It provoked instant illness: nausea, vomiting, and breathlessness were at the top of the list. Notably, the Slenderman is very often described as exuding odors— sometimes of a nauseous and foul nature and, on other occasions, of an oddly entrancing type. Mind-controlling, even, it's fair to say. Urban Raef was practically rendered helpless by the smell. Meanwhile, his wife, in bed, found herself temporarily unable to move. In moments, however, the curious event was over.

This sounds very much like a condition known as "sleep-paralysis," which many students of the supernatural believe are caused by the presence and actions of paranormal creatures invading peoples' minds and homes as they sleep. The official term for this undeniably frightening phenomenon is

Hypnagogia. Basically, it describes the hazy and mysterious period between wakefulness and the sleep state; a period that may be dominated by a wide and infinitely varied body of alarming and weird experiences. Unusual voices, very often speaking in unintelligible tones, are commonplace, as are sightings of floating heads and bizarre creatures ranging from extraterrestrials to demons, monsters, and ghosts. The big question is whether experiences such as mine, and those of many others, are solely provoked by the internal intricacies of the human mind, or by something external and supernatural that can psychically invade us while we are in the sleep state—such as the Slenderman.

"THERE IS NO DOUBT THAT A GAS MANIAC EXISTS"

Barely 48 hours after the Raef family was descended upon by the mad and malevolent thing with a penchant for gas, the Kearney family found itself on the receiving end of a visit of the most unwelcome type. And they were hit hard. It was at around 11 p.m. when Mrs. Kearney was lying in bed, dozing, and felt a terrifying paralysis slowly creep up her legs. As the paralysis increased, a sweet smell—almost sickening in nature—completely enveloped the bedroom. She screamed for her sister, Martha, who also found herself overwhelmed by the almost-incapacitating smell. Who, or what, was responsible for the two attacks? An answer, of sorts, came when Mrs. Kearney's husband, Bert (a cab driver) came home not long after his night shift was over. Just as he reached the family home, Bert saw, on the front yard and peering through the window of their bedroom, *a tall, thin man dressed in black*. He was gone by the time Bert had jumped out of his car and raced in the direction of the "man."

In no time at all, and as a result of the profoundly weird nature of the attacks, the police and even J. Edgar Hoover's Federal Bureau of Investigation were on the case. As panic quickly gripped the townsfolk of Mattoon, the then-Commissioner of Health, Thomas V. Wright, issued the release of the following statement:

> There is no doubt that a gas maniac exists and has made a number of attacks. But many of the reported attacks are nothing more than hysteria. Fear of the gas man is entirely out of proportion to the menace of the relatively harmless gas he is spraying. The whole town is sick with hysteria (Taylor, 2011).

The town was sick with something else too: out-of-control fear.

Theories for who, or what, the Mad Gasser was abounded. The suspects included a local young man named Farley Llewellyn. He was someone who knew several of the victims and who had a fascination for chemistry. Nothing incriminating was found, however, to *conclusively* say that Llewellyn was the mastermind behind the attacks.

Robbers, teenage kids, and even aliens, have all since been put forward as potential candidates for the gruesome Gasser. The answer to the riddle? There is none. Only an abundance of theories, many of them supernaturally themed.

Yet again, we see a mysterious and unsettling affair involving a gaunt, tall figure in black, and who—just like H.P. Lovecraft's Night-Gaunts and the Slenderman—had the ability to invade the sleeping-states of those unlucky souls who lived within the homes the Mad Gasser chose to target. *And from whom Eric Knudsen drew inspiration.*

MEN IN BLACK SUITS

The Slenderman is not the only menacing creature that wears a black suit. Make mention of the sinister MIB to most people and they will likely think of Will Smith and Tommy Lee Jones. Indeed, there is no doubt that the hugely popular trilogy of *Men in Black* movies has cemented the image of the MIB in the minds of millions all across the planet. The movies have achieved something else, too: They have ensured that many people assume the Men in Black are the secret employees of an equally secret government agency which investigates the UFO phenomenon in stealth. The reality, however, is far different. It's a fact that the overwhelming majority of people who have reported encounters with the MIB describe something far removed from the worlds of government, the military, or the intelligence community. *Their encounters are far more Slenderman-like.*

In the vast majority of MIB confrontations, the eyewitnesses describe the ominous, black-suited visitors as being pale-faced. They are often emaciated in the extreme and very tall. They typically hide their eyes behind large, wraparound, black sunglasses. There is a very good reason for this: Their eyes are often described as being larger than normal. Or, as one witness worded it, "He had huge, thyroid eyes." They typically surface at night, when the skies are dark and the sun has set, and they use what can only be categorized as a form of "mind-control" to force their victims to open the door and invite them—not unlike the actions and tales of equally pale, black-clothed vampires of centuries long gone (Redfern, 2011).

As all of the above demonstrate, there are strong indications that the real MIB (as opposed to those created by Hollywood) are not even human. On top of that, many people who have been visited and threatened by the MIB describe how the MIB had the ability to drain them of energy, and even to provoke violent poltergeist-like activity in the home. Strange odors, such as those of a sulfur-like nature, are reported when and where the MIB are lurking around. Cases of people falling seriously ill—physically and mentally—after being in close proximity to the Men in Black are not unknown. And, on numerous occasions, people have spoken of how the MIB invaded their dreams. Just like the Slenderman.

Let's now take a closer look at a few of those similarities.

Silencing a saucer-seeker

There is no doubt that the one person, more than any other, who brought the Men in Black to the attention of the UFO research community in the early 1950s was Albert Bender. He was a devotee of all things Ufological, a big fan of the writings of H.P. Lovecraft, and someone who created a successful UFO research group called the International Flying Saucer Bureau. At least, it was successful until late one night in 1953. That was when a trio of gaunt, emotionless Men in Black materialized in Bender's bedroom, in his hometown of Bridgeport, Connecticut. Echoing the saga of the Mad Gasser of Mattoon a decade earlier, Bender was overcome by a powerful smell of brimstone and plunged into a dizzy, light-headed state that left him feeling distinctly ill. Bender was almost immediately rendered immobile on the bed.

The semi-physical Men in Black telepathically warned Bender off his UFO research. It didn't take long before Bender got the bleak message. He quickly quit Ufology, only briefly returning to the scene in the early 1960s to write a book on his encounters with the MIB (*Flying Saucers and the Three Men*) and then leaving the subject behind him for good. Bender died in 2016 at the age of 94. Had he not quit the UFO scene when he did, and instead continued to be supernaturally attacked by the Men in Black, one has to wonder if Bender would have come close to living to that impressive old age.

Like so many witnesses to the Slenderman, and also echoing the experiences of H.P. Lovecraft with the highly dangerous Night-Gaunts, Albert Bender found to his eternal horror that the Men in Black had the ability to penetrate his dreams and manipulate them into absolute horror stories. There is also the issue of the height of the MIB and their ubiquitous black suits. Those issues, too, mirror the physical appearance of the Slenderman, as we'll now see.

MIB: Tall, tentacled, and terrifying

Harold T. Wilkins was a UFO researcher who, in the 1950s, wrote several books on UFOs, including what was certainly his most well-known and popular title, *Flying Saucers on the Attack*. Wilkins was also someone who found himself on the receiving end of a number of Men in Black–themed reports. One such report described certain, uncanny events that occurred in Los Angeles, California, in 1953 and that are highly relevant to the theme of this book. Wilkins's source of the story insisted on anonymity, but revealed that it all revolved around a particular attorney's office in downtown Los Angeles. According to Wilkins's informant, a pair of men dressed in black appeared at the building one evening and demanded to see the director of the company. The pair insisted that they be hired to investigate recent reports of missing persons in the city. Those mind-controlling skills of the MIB ensured that they were quickly, albeit briefly, hired. But there was something about the pair that was just not right. Actually, there were a few things that were just plain wrong. *Horribly* wrong.

Those employees who caught sight of the MIB (who spent most of their time locked in one particular office and who spoke with practically no one) said they were very skinny and were both in excess of six-and-a-half feet in height. They were described as having strange hands and fingers—the latter being extremely long and rubbery, as if they lacked joints and bones. On one occasion, according to Wilkins's notes, one of the staff saw the fingers of one of the MIB stretch to lengths of around eight or nine inches, something which, she added, made the man's hands appear to resemble huge tentacles. In days, the MIB were gone, never to be seen again. Of course, we should not understate the importance of the revelation that one of the tall and skinny Men in Black had tentacle-like fingers. We are clearly, *right now*, deep within the absolute black heart of Slenderman territory.

Today, there are hundreds of such MIB reports on record. Hardly any of them have even a remote bearing on the "secret agent" angle, as portrayed in the *Men in Black* movies. In contrast, many of the MIB reports mirror encounters with the Slenderman, and particularly so regarding the "dream-invading" abilities, the mind-controlling skills, and the supernatural powers of both. And let us not forget that both are skinny and tall, and wear nothing but black suits. No wonder the Men in Black were part and parcel of the Slenderman's development.

"TWO-DIMENSIONAL HUMAN SHAPES"

Now, it's time to take a look at yet another of Knudsen's inspirations for the Slenderman, the Shadow People, which come across as appropriately shadowy equivalents of the Men in Black, hence their name. And just like the MIB and H.P. Lovecraft's Night-Gaunts, the Shadow People are definitive dream-penetrators. Natalia Kuna says that the Shadow People are "…conscious, intelligent, interdimensional beings that can move into our dimension…. Mostly they are interdimensional beings that shapeshift into various forms and move back and forth between dimensions and figurations, but some are possibly demonic creatures or even evil spirits or entities. Some are extremely evil and predatory…." (Kuna, 2017).

Jason Offutt, an acknowledged expert on the Shadow People notes:

> People across the globe have reported seeing these black, two-dimensional, human shapes stalk the bedrooms and hallways of their homes. Sometimes these Shadow People ignore you, sometimes they pay all too much attention, but they are always sinister (Offutt, 2009).

In light of the that thought, it's easy to see why the Shadow People came to impact upon the creation of, and the imagery associated with, the Slenderman.

A WINGED MONSTER AND COUNTLESS DEATHS

Finally, there is the matter of yet another strange creature that has become legendary within the worlds of both fact and fiction. Its name is Mothman. It, too, played a role in the development of the Slenderman character, as Eric Knudsen has confirmed. Between the final weeks of 1966 and Christmas 1967, the residents of Point Pleasant, West Virginia, found themselves in a collective state of fear when sightings occurred of an ominous beast soaring across the dark skies of the town. Witnesses told the media and the local police that the creature had its lair deep somewhere within the dense woods surrounding an old, abandoned TNT storage area of the military—surely the perfect hiding place for a monster to lurk in.

Many locals described the beast as a dark-skinned, winged humanoid with bright red eyes. *Blazing* might be a far more apt word to use. As sightings of the Mothman increased, a dark and foreboding atmosphere quickly fell upon Point Pleasant and its residents. That atmosphere of dread reached its absolute pinnacle on December 15, 1967. It was on the evening in question that the town's old

Silver Bridge collapsed into the churning waters of the Ohio River. Forty-six people lost their lives. Today, there are two primary theories for the presence of the Mothman: It was the cause of the tragedy and it was akin to a Grim Reaper–type character, or that it was there to warn people of the looming disaster, rather than personally provoke it.

Of the 46 dead, two were never found, lost to the darkness of that December night and the churning, wild waters of the river. One of them was a young girl. Thus, we see a parallel to the Slenderman affair: A child is taken by a monster and never seen again. Things didn't end there, though. The catalog of deaths had barely begun. Although things were quiet for several decades, in the late 1990s the specter of the Mothman resurfaced.

THE DEATHS CONTINUE AND ESCALATE

Jim Keith was a noted conspiracy theorist who died under extremely questionable and dubious circumstances in September 1999 after attending the annual Burning Man event in Nevada's Black Rock Desert. In his 1997 book *Casebook of the Men in Black*, Keith focused much of his attention on the Mothman saga, as well as the timely presence in Point Pleasant of the notorious MIB. Some said that Keith got a little too close to the truth of the Men in Black/Mothman connection and paid for it with his life. He was just 49 years old when he passed. It wasn't long before Keith's publisher and buddy, Ron Bonds, was dead too, also under controversial circumstances. Notably, back in 1991 Bonds had republished John Keel's classic book on the 1966–1967 events that went down in Point Pleasant: *The Mothman Prophecies*, which was first published in 1975. Interest in Keel's book reached stratospheric proportions when, in 2002, it was turned into a big-bucks movie starring Richard Gere and Laura Linney. That's when the deaths began to kick in big time.

The movie hit cinemas in the United States on January 25, 2002. On that very day a funeral was taking place. It was the funeral of one of the early witnesses to the Mothman, a man named Charlie Mallette. Less than seven days after Mallette's death, there were five fatalities in Point Pleasant, all as a result of car accidents. Weeks later, Ted Tannebaum, the executive producer of *The Mothman Prophecies*, died from cancer.

In much the same way that the premiere of *The Mothman Prophecies* movie in the United States was blighted by tragedy and death, exactly the same can be said about the day on which the movie hit cinemas on the other side of the world, specifically in Australia. On May 23, 2002, a teenage boy from Fort Smith, Arkansas, named Aaron Rebsamen killed himself. His father was William Rebsamen, a skilled artist whose atmospheric imagery of the Mothman can be seen on the front cover of Loren Coleman's 2002 book, *Mothman and Other Curious Encounters*.

The author in the domain of the Mothman. *Nick Redfern, 2014.*

A month after the death of Aaron Rebsamen, a woman named Sherry Marie Yearsley was murdered; her body was dumped near an old railroad in Sparks, Nevada. She and Ron Bonds, who, as noted, had republished *The Mothman Prophecies*, had dated for a while. Then, as 2002 came to its close, Mothman investigator Susan Wilcox passed away from cancer. Six months later, Jessica Kaplan, who worked on *The Mothman Prophecies* film, died in a plane crash. The acclaimed actor Alan Bates, who had a starring role in *The Mothman Prophecies*, was dead shortly before the end of 2003. Then, in July 2004, Jennifer Barrett-Pellington died.

She was the wife of Mark Pellington, who was none other than the director of *The Mothman Prophecies.*

As all of these examples demonstrate, taking the lead from potentially dangerous and supernatural beings like Mothman can be hazardous in the extreme, and particularly so when one embarks on a path toward creating an Internet meme of a horrendous type. It's at this point we have to take note of the words of the aforementioned actor, the late Alan Bates. In *The Mothman Prophecies*, Bates's character Alexander Leek tells Richard Gere's John Klein: "When you noticed these things, they noticed that you noticed them."

Leek, based on John Keel, was explaining to Klein (also based on Keel) how, when one pursues the likes of Mothman—or maybe even just *thinks* about it—the entity has a form of "supernatural radar" or "alarm" that alerts the beast to the fact that someone is pursuing or focusing on it. John Keel experienced this very phenomenon on countless occasions when he was prowling around 1960s-era Point Pleasant after dark.

Just maybe, when Eric Knudsen took so much inspiration from emaciated, supernatural creatures dressed in black—some utterly faceless, and others with tentacle- and octopus-like digits and arms—those same creatures noticed *him* and decided to play a few warped and tormenting games of their very own variety. Turning the tables, perhaps. Knudsen certainly let the Slenderman loose on the Internet, but was his inspiration guided by certain things he had read or by things from other realms, rather than by his imagination? The supernatural archetypes for Knudsen's unholy offspring may have taken things to a whole new level and created a horrific and *real* monstrous chimera for the 21st century, something that was part-MIB, part-Night-Gaunt, part-Mad Gasser, and part-supernatural shadow: the Slenderman.

That very same chimera may have cruelly manipulated the minds of a pair of girls from Wisconsin who, in May 2014, attempted to perform a terrible sacrifice in the name of the Slenderman.

6

"CONSUMED BY THE SLENDERMAN"

Waukesha, a city of approximately 70,000 people, is located in a pleasant suburb of Milwaukee, Wisconsin. Its origins date back to the early part of the 19th century, when settlers from Maine, Connecticut, and Vermont put down roots in the area, ensuring that it would soon become a bustling hive of activity. It's a city noted for its picturesque buildings, its close proximity to the huge and equally picturesque Fox River, and the fact that it was the birthplace of the late guitar legend Les Paul. Waukesha does, however, have its dark side.

In May 2014, Waukesha hit the headlines in a way that few, if any, could ever have anticipated: The dark and foreboding specter of the Slenderman descended on the city in just about the worst way possible. In many respects, the city and its people have still not forgotten the horrific events that put them firmly on the map. Chances are, given the tragic and disturbing nature of the affair, they never will forget. In a truly chilling fashion, Waukesha became inextricably linked to the Internet's most fearsome and feared monster.

Saturday, May 31st was the day on which Waukesha made what began as local news. In quick time, however, it became nationwide news. Then, ultimately and hardly surprisingly, it became nothing less than absolute *worldwide* news. None of that news, however, was of a positive nature. On the morning in question, two young local girls, Anissa Weier and Morgan Geyser, viciously attacked another girl, Payton Leutner, a school friend of the pair whose nickname was Bella. It was all done in the name of the Slenderman, as incredible and baffling as that might sound. Such was the violent nature of the assault—an attack that left Leutner seriously injured—it sent shockwaves all across the city. The incident did something else, too: When the media quickly latched onto the news, the result was that millions of people were very quickly exposed to the phenomenon of the Slenderman, which is an important issue when it comes to how and under what circumstances the monster may have achieved a degree of life as a Tulpa.

How could such a terrible and terrifying thing have occurred? And why, exactly? The story sounds like something straight out of the firmly fiction-based tales that surfaced in the wake of the emergence of the Slenderman on the Internet in the summer of 2009, except for one thing: This was the *real* world, the one in which you and I live. Not one dominated by dark, online fantasies. The line between reality and fiction had just become even more entangled; this time in a horrifically surreal fashion.

PLANNING A SACRIFICE

Anissa Weier and Morgan Geyser, who were both 12 years of age at the time of the attack on their former friend, had an overriding obsession with the Slenderman phenomenon, having been exposed to it after checking out the *Creepypasta Wiki* website. The site has a section devoted specifically to the Slenderman which, in part, states: "Despite the fact that it is rumored [the Slenderman] kills children almost exclusively, it is difficult to say whether or not his only objective is slaughter" ("The Slender Man," 2017).

Creepypasta Wiki further notes that the Slenderman is often encountered in suburban woods, is seen with significantly sized groups of youngsters, and preys on children. Notably, the issues of children, death, and woods (which Weier and Geyser specifically learned about from

Creepypasta Wiki) were parts of the appalling May 31st attack that almost took the life of Payton Leutner.

In the wake of the attack, "Mr. CreepyPasta," described as the "king" of the Slenderman stories that can be found on YouTube, said:

> I guess *Creepypasta* is dangerous to a degree if we're talking about the Slenderman stabbing…. When you're talking about entertainment, you have to understand that it's fiction. Just because it's on the Internet doesn't mean it's real. The danger here is that *Creepypasta* is entertainment largely aimed at kids and teenagers (Gaudette, 2017).

Little did anyone know at the time, but, after checking out *Creepypasta Wiki*, both Weier and Geyser were, bit by bit, sucked deep into the dark and malevolence-filled world of the Slenderman. And their obsessions only grew and grew in truly alarming ways. Interestingly, Matt Hrodey, in a January 2016 article titled "In the Woods," which appeared in the *Milwaukee Magazine*, wrote the following: "Unlike Morgan, Anissa experienced little in the way of hallucinations leading up to the attacks. Sometime after she began reading *Creepypasta*, she started to see a dark figure in the wooded areas that her school bus passed, a form 'in the branches,'" something which a Milwaukee-based psychologist, Anthony Jurek confirmed. Jurek, in his opinion, suggested that what she had experienced was a "visual illusion," rather than a "defined hallucination" (Hrodey, 2016).

The night before the lives of three 12 year olds were radically and forever altered was, rather ironically, a completely normal one. The girls, who all attended Horning Middle School in Waukesha, had a sleepover for Morgan's birthday. It was a fun evening that gave not even a single sign or inkling of the mayhem that loomed large on the horizon; the three played a computer game and then spent time at the local Skateland. Even the following morning started out in a completely down-to-earth fashion: The girls all hung out together and ate a breakfast of donuts and strawberries. That air of pleasant normality changed radically a couple of hours later. Unbridled savagery was very soon to be the order of the day. Weier and Geyser were gearing up to sacrifice their ill-fated friend to their *new* best friend.

A FRENZIED ATTACK

It was just before 10 a.m. when absolute carnage erupted. Geyser had taken a five-inch-long steak knife from her home and she and Weier callously lured Leutner to David's Park, a nearby wooded area, with the intention of killing her. Leutner, of course, had absolutely no idea of what the pair had in store for her. If she had, she surely would not have hung around. She would have fled the area, likely never,

ever to return. Unfortunately, that's not what happened. In a truly nightmarish situation, and in a tree-shrouded portion of the park off of Big Bend Road, the attack began. However, matters did not go exactly to plan. For Leutner, that turned out to be a blessing and almost a miracle.

Anissa, at the very last minute, found that she couldn't go through with the attack. It was all left to Morgan to do the dirty and diabolical work. She savagely plunged the knife into Leutner's arms, legs, and body *19 times*. Anissa merely stood there, watching, completely and utterly transfixed. The girls then guided their victim further into the trees, essentially to try and ensure that she would not be seen by anyone and could not call out for help. Payton then collapsed to the ground. Anissa and Morgan quickly fled the area, cleaned themselves up at a local Wal-Mart, and were content in their beliefs that by killing—*sacrificing*, effectively—their schoolmate they would be granted entrance to the Slenderman's personal abode. It was said to be a spatial, large house hidden deep in the heart of the Nicolet National Forest.

Planning a rendezvous in the woods

The idea was for the two girls, after the attack, to head off to the forest and make their careful and stealthy way to the creepy old mansion of the Slenderman. All that the Slenderman needed from the girls was a sacrificial offering. And he now had that specific offering, in the form of

Leutner. Well, no, actually, he didn't. In fact, quite the opposite was the case. Incredibly, and against all odds, the 19 stab wounds did not kill Payton. When Anissa and Morgan fled the park, the girls had no idea Payton was destined to survive their violent attack. Despite being seriously injured, Payton still had the guts and the determination to beat the Grim Reaper—and the tentacle-waving monster in black, too. She slowly crawled out of the woods and, using up most of her rapidly dwindling energy, managed to make it to a stretch of sidewalk in the park. As luck or fate would have it, a passing cyclist caught sight of her and, shocked to the core, quickly called emergency services. She whispered to the cyclist that she had been stabbed. In quick time, thankfully, those same emergency services arrived at the park. They were as shocked as the cyclist was by the bloody scene before them. When Payton was asked who stabbed her, she replied in gasping tones that it was her best friends.

Only when she was rushed to a nearby hospital did the sheer and graphic nature of the attack become all too clear: There were significant cuts to the skin, damage to several of her organs (her liver was pierced, as was her stomach and pancreas), and a major artery to her heart had narrowly missed being sliced wide open (had the artery been penetrated, it would have ensured a quick and horrific death for the young girl). The sheer shock of the attack caused Payton to lose both her vision and her voice. Thankfully, they quickly returned.

Fortunately, she was able to provide law-enforcement personnel with the names of the girls and police sought out and apprehended Anissa and Morgan. The girls were found walking on nearby Interstate 94, reportedly on their way to the Slenderman's abode: the mysterious, old mansion in the heart of the forest. By the time the police were on the scene, the girls had managed to travel approximately five miles on foot, stopping only at a Steinhafels store, where they grabbed both drinks and food for the rest of the journey. It was at the ramp from Highway F to I-94 that they were finally caught.

The police drove to the Geyser residence and explained that there had been an incident: One girl was injured and Morgan and Anissa were not with her, which didn't really explain anything to the frantic parents. They finally found out what had happened. Of course, the parents of all three girls were devastated. Angie Geyser, Morgan's mother, said that on arriving at the police station and having been told what happened, "I sobbed. I ran to the bathroom and threw up. It didn't seem possible" (Vielmetti, 2016).

It was when the pair was in custody that the near-unimaginable story of what happened came tumbling out. It was a story that even chilled the police to their collective bones. If the cops thought they had seen and heard everything, they were very wrong. For the officers assigned to investigate the attack, it was completely new territory. It was highly dangerous territory, too.

LAW ENFORCEMENT AND THE SLENDERMAN

Recordings of the police interviews with the two girls revealed that they knew all about the Slenderman phenomenon: Anissa, for example, gave a disturbingly matter-of-fact description of the Slenderman to the authorities, noting the lack of eyes, nose, and mouth on his pale face, his black suit, the monstrous tentacles that were attached to his back, and his giant height. The police were also told that the Slenderman had the ability to read the girls' minds and even possessed the power of teleportation. Everything was carefully chronicled by law enforcement agents as the strange and unsettling tale unfolded. A real-life *X-File*? To be sure, yes. Morgan revealed to the police that she was deeply afraid of what might have happened to her and Anissa if the sacrifice didn't go ahead as planned: She feared that failure would provoke the Slenderman to turn the tables on *them* and come after *her* family.

There's no doubt that Geyser fully believed in the existence of the Slenderman. When the authorities asked her if she really believed that her own family would suffer if the attack on Payton Leutner had not gone forward, she told them: "Well, yeah. He's six to 14 feet tall, has no face, and always wears a red tie. I was really scared. He could kill my whole family in three seconds" (Vielmetti, 2015).

As for Payton, when she was well enough to speak with police, she said that she felt Morgan should go to jail for the rest of her life. No one could blame her for thinking that. On the matter of Anissa, however, Payton was of the opinion that she should have a shorter sentence. This was due to the fact that although she was certainly directly involved in instigating the attack, Anissa did not physically take part in it—something that suggests Payton had a degree of sympathy for her former friend, despite the secret and savage plot launched against her. This was in stark contrast to the reactions and responses of Anissa and Morgan, who the authorities said showed not even a single shred of remorse for what they had done. They didn't even appear to have a full understanding of the gravity of their actions—or of the implications for what lied ahead for them.

As time went on, further eye-opening data surfaced that shed a great deal of light on the girls and their characters. For example, Morgan's mother recalled the time when they watched the 1942 Walt Disney movie *Bambi*. When Bambi's mother was shot dead, Geyser did not break out in tears, or respond in an emotion-filled fashion, as a youngster might very well have been expected to do. Morgan's mother admitted that she found this lack of emotion to be somewhat unusual.

THE SLENDERMAN TELEVISION DOCUMENTARY

In January 2017 a television documentary on the Geyser-Weier-Leutner affair was broadcast on HBO. Its title was *Beware the Slenderman*. It was, and still remains, a deeply powerful and disturbing piece of work that skillfully captured the events in question and the devastating effects that the attack had on all three families involved. Parents in tears and in states of turmoil, lives irreparably ripped and torn apart, a pet cat pining and faithfully searching for its now-incarcerated friend, and endless questions about how on earth such a terrible thing could have occurred, were just a few of the issues graphically presented to the viewer. *Beware the Slenderman* brought other notable issues to light, too. None of them can be deemed positive in nature.

One of the more thought-provoking revelations that surfaced in the documentary was that, although Anissa and Morgan largely learned about the Slenderman from *Creepypasta Wiki*, Anissa had dreams of the Slenderman at the very young age of three years old, which was almost a decade *before* Payton Leutner was nearly killed and several years prior to the Slenderman surfacing online in 2009. So, we have an example of the Slenderman having some degree of existence before Eric Knudsen came on to the scene.

Morgan's mother revealed in the *Beware the Slenderman* documentary that her daughter had told her how ghosts apparently appeared in her bedroom at night; that they pulled on her hair and bit her body. Was all of this evidence that the pair had been plagued by a *real* Slenderman, rather than having been guided by an obsession with an Internet fantasy that had spiraled chaotically out of control? This eye-opening issue of Slenderman sightings *pre*-2009 is something we'll come back to in a later chapter.

Beware the Slenderman also chronicled the court hearings that followed the girls' arrests. They were somewhat odd, in the sense that the matter of the Slenderman himself—what he was said to be and the nature of his actions and motivations—were discussed almost as much as the attempted killing of Leutner.

Two girls go to court; another one thrives

As for what fate has in store for Anissa and Morgan, well, that is something which still remains very much unknown and in a state of deep imbalance. Morgan has been diagnosed with schizophrenia, a condition that her father Matt also has. In Morgan's case, it is specifically referred to as Childhood Onset Schizophrenia. After her arrest, such was Morgan's fraught state of mind that she spent time in the Wisconsin-based Winnebago Mental Health Institute. Even her mother Angie said that Morgan was "floridly psychotic for 19 months." Attempts to have the girls brought before Juvenile Court have, thus far, failed. Wisconsin law allows for anyone over the age of 10 to be tried as an adult, which is exactly where things currently are for Morgan and Anissa. The case continues. For Payton Leutner, however, things are definitely on the up (Vielmetti, 2016).

In January 2017, WISN Milwaukee news ran an article titled "Slender Man Stabbing Victim Thriving, Family Says." The writer of the article, Nick Borh, noted: "A girl who barely survived being attacked by two friends is now thriving, taking AP classes in school and has joined her French club on a class trip to Canada, a family spokesman said" (Bohr, 2017).

"There's some normalcy, after this horrific premeditated crime, and we're just very proud of her," said that same spokesman, Steve Lyons (Ibid.).

The latest news on the Slenderman stabbings

On April 13, 2017, the media revealed a new development in the case. It was on that same day that Morgan Geyser found herself in court yet again—this time for what was described as a status conference, something initiated to arrange a specific date for the trial. Morgan's trial was pushed back by 14 days specifically so that Anissa's trial could proceed in an uninterrupted fashion. The court also arranged for a questionnaire to be created, one that could be sent to all of the possible jurors in the case. Anthony Cotton,

Morgan's attorney, explained the reasons for this particular action: "The whole idea is that she'll have a fairer jury because we'll have more information about the jurors. It probably will not speed up the process in terms of selecting a jury quicker" (DeLong & Taylor, 2017).

It was estimated that the potential jurors would receive their questionnaires by July 2017.

It's intriguing to note that Morgan's attorney put in a request that the jury specifically *not* be selected from Waukesha County, which is where the attack occurred and where all three girls were from. The reason and rationale for all of this? The huge amount of local media publicity afforded the attack and the subsequent events. The concern was that a local jury might be influenced by all of the media coverage in their hometown rather than taking an impartial look at the evidence in the case. Cotton also noted that the incident had been reported at a worldwide level. The judge overseeing the case stated that media-driven publicity—excessive or otherwise—was not inflammatory, was based strictly on the public record, and was not of the likes of hearsay. Geyser had a motion hearing in July, and another status conference in the later part of August. Her trial was planned for October 16th, 2017. As for Weier, on April 28th, she was destined for a status conference herself.

Then, on June 8th, 2017, it was revealed by the media that lawyers for the girls were seeking to determine precisely

The Slenderman: A bedroom invader. *Simon Wyatt, 2017.*

how much potential jurors already know about the stabbing and the Slenderman controversy. Again, this was driven by concerns revolving around the extent to which knowledge of both issues might bias the jury's thoughts on the attack.

Matters came to their peak when, in August 2017, Anissa pleaded guilty to attempted second-degree homicide as a result of mental illness; although in the following month, the majority of the jury in Anissa's case found her not guilty because of her psychological state. She will likely spend around three years in a mental health facility. As for Morgan, she pleaded guilty to attempted first-degree murder. Judge Michael Bohren, however, found Morgan not guilty due to her mental state, which means that not being found criminally responsible, she will be confined in an institution, rather than in a jail. Although Payton Leutner's family was not happy with this situation, they accepted it.

As for that piece of woodland in which very lucky Payton nearly lost her life, it has since been razed to the ground. Hopefully, that welcome action will help to wipe out at least *some* of the memories of that terrible day on which a young girl—one with her whole life in front of her—almost died because of her former friends' disturbing obsession with the Slenderman; an obsession that now has two girls pondering deeply on their futures and another eternally thankful that she didn't lose her life.

Reflecting on all of this, Waukesha Chief of Police Russell P. Jack told the media: "The Internet can be full of dark and wicked things" (Pearce, 2014).

It can, indeed.

"IT WAS THEIR SECRET; THEIR LITTLE CLUB"

Finally, for this chapter, at least, it's worth taking note of the words of someone who has studied the Slenderman phenomenon extensively, and who can also offer personal insight into how incredibly deeply children have become fixated on the Slenderman and the legends that surround him.

Olav Phillips is the publisher of a popular magazine that delves deep into the world of all-things conspiratorial and mysterious. Its highly appropriate title is *Paranoia Magazine*. The Fall 2014 issue of the magazine gave considerable page space to the many and various controversies surrounding the Slenderman and included David Weatherly's article, "The Tendrils of the Slenderman," Clyde Lewis's "Slenderman: Proof of a Modern Tulpa," and "Slenderman Becomes Too Real," which was penned by Loren and Jenny Coleman.

Phillips, having a deep interest in the overall phenomenon of the Slenderman, has made valuable observations and comments on the way in which the infamous creature has caught the attention of children in general and of one in particular: his very own son. Having a young child—a son with a fascination for the Slenderman—Phillips is in a prime position to address this specific aspect of the enigma. He recalls:

I remember speaking to my son and asked him if he had ever heard of the Slenderman—this was when I got into it, which was just a few years ago. He was about eight at the time and he gets real scared and he just says: "What?" He asked me: "Where did you hear about that?" I said, "On the Net." He was asking really softly, almost secretly, like it was something for him and his friends, but not for the grown-ups. It was *their* secret; *their* little club. Not mine (Redfern-Phillips, interview, 2017).

Phillips reveals something eye-opening in the extreme:

In my son's elementary school, Slenderman was like their version of Bloody Mary. They were fascinated by it, but scared and mortified, too. Even in grade two and three, my son said the kids were consumed by the Slenderman thing; *completely* consumed by it. With my son and his friends, there's a lot of secrecy and paranoia with the Slenderman; you can't tell people about this. They feel comfortable talking about it with each other, because that's their cohort. But when I come in—and I'm the old guy—I'm not supposed to know about that. That's how they see it, I think (Ibid.).

And just like his son, Phillips was drawn to the Slenderman like a moth to a flame. He says of this almost hypnotic issue: "About a month after me and my son had that conversation was when the girls stabbed their friend. I had to investigate it; it became like an addiction. I can't sit there and do nothing about it; it was very strange" (Ibid.). Phillips adds:

> At first, I believed it was a hundred percent horseshit, just made-up stories and nothing else. But, then, after me and my son talked about it, it struck me that there was so much fear in my son's elementary school, and the beliefs they had in the Slenderman were fairly complicated. That was when I started to think it had gone from this totally made-up story to a Tulpa—manifested by millions of children across the United States and around the world.
>
> The imagery and the name definitely had a lot to do with it for my son, I think; even for me. When we were kids, we were all afraid of the boogeyman: the guy under the bed or in the closet. But, you didn't really have an image to go with it. I'm 42 now, so we didn't have anything that visually manifested for us back then, in the 1980s. And we didn't have anything like the Internet—no pictures of the boogeyman to look at. And information was much slower to spread, too. The Slenderman thing was different: It became a meme. There were stories, images online. The way my son got it, it was like how the boogeyman story was told to me, but in a bigger 21st-century context (Ibid.).

7

"WAUKESHA REMINDS ME OF A NIGHTMARE ON ELM STREET"

ne of the lesser known aspects of the Slenderman phenomenon is its connection to the strange issue of what are known as *synchronicities*. Writer Paul Levy says that synchronicities are "…those moments of 'meaningful coincidence' when the boundary dissolves between the inner and the outer. At the synchronistic moment, just like a dream, our internal, subjective state appears, as if materialized in, as and through the outside world" (Levy, 2010).

And there is this from the Personal Tao website: "Synchronicity is a term that came into popular use through

Swiss psychotherapist Carl Jung. In his life and during sessions with clients he experienced 'meaningful coincidences' where two or more signs, that occurred randomly, were also connected by meaning (not by cause) ("Synchronicity and Signs," 2017).

In relation to the Slenderman, the nature of the synchronicities range from the strange to the downright sinister. Most of them revolve around the May 31, 2014 attack in Waukesha, Wisconsin. There is one aspect of the Slenderman issue—in relation to the attack—that is barely ever touched upon by commentators on the creature and its actions, which is, admittedly, baffling. A strong case can be made that it relates directly to the events which occurred on May 31, 2014, when Morgan Geyser and Anissa Weier tried to kill Payton Leutner. But in a very odd way, which is so very often typical of synchronicities, they are seldom easy to fully decipher and understand.

On the very night before the knife attack occurred, *Coast to Coast AM*'s host Dave Schrader introduced a guest named Bill Murphy, the host of the SyFy Channel's *Fact or Faked: The Paranormal Files*. A significant portion of the interview was devoted to the issue of how certain ghostly phenomena might be Tulpa-based in nature—a theory that we have already addressed to explain how and why the Slenderman came into being in the real world. The show had barely begun when Schrader brought up with Murphy the matter of the Slenderman. Was it possible,

Schrader wanted to know, that the Slenderman was indeed a thought-form? Murphy gave Schrader an interesting reply. Before getting to the heart of the issue, though, Murphy provided for listeners the background of the Slenderman controversy, such as its appearance (tall and spindly) and how it targeted children, particularly so in playgrounds. Murphy also touched on the issue of the Photoshopped images of the Slenderman, noting that this aspect of the phenomenon was in no way connected to hoaxing, but was much more akin to what he correctly termed "a social experiment" ("How the Living Influence Hauntings," 2014).

Dave Schrader posed interesting questions: "Did the Slenderman always exist and we peeled back those layers and now people can see him, because we're aware of him? Or did we create something that has taken on a life of its own?" (Ibid.).

Murphy's reply was fascinating. He explained to Schrader and to *Coast to Coast AM's* huge audience that when people go online and enter the term "Slenderman," it may well amount to a "reflection of a collective consciousness of what people want to know around the world" (Ibid.).

Murphy speculated that perhaps a group thought, or even a *global* thought, may well have brought the Slenderman to some degree of what passes for life. In view of this theory, one has to wonder if the specific discussion of the Slenderman as a thought-form, *just one night before* the stabbing in Waukesha occurred, gave further life and power to the Slenderman character, which *already* had its grips in Anissa Weier and Morgan Geyser. On this same issue, it's important to note that because the show was such a long one, the interview between Schrader and Murphy actually continued into the early hours of May 31st, the very day of the attack. That *Coast to Coast AM* has such a phenomenally massive number of listeners may also have had a bearing on how and why the Slenderman controversy reached its terrible peak only a handful of hours after the show aired. More listeners equals more believers. More believers equals a more powerful, dangerous, and corporeal Slenderman.

COMMENTS FROM A LISTENER

Although the *Coast to Coast AM* show was broadcast live on the night of the 30th and spilled over into the early hours of the day on which Payton Leutner almost lost her life, the episodes are quickly archived. One of the people who listened to the archived show on the Slenderman, on the very morning of the attack, was Allison Jornlin. When I spoke with Allison, specifically to interview her for this book, she pointed out something to me: I had contacted her on the third anniversary of the Geyser-Weier attack, May 31, 2017, which was kind of odd and synchronistic. Jornlin's words follow:

In the *C2C* show from the night before, Bill Murphy and Dave Schrader discuss Slenderman specifically and how he may manifest as a Tulpa because so many people are feeding him energy. So I'm listening to this on the day of the Slenderman stabbing and only later find out that it happened. There may be an interesting connection here you'd want to explore. Were the perpetrators listening to the show the night before? Did the energy of the show with its huge listenership help cause what happened? Or is it just an extraordinary coincidence? (Jornlin, 2017).

It likely was *not* a coincidence, as the synchronicities continued to pile up. Allison Jornlin's brother Mike Huberty happens to run ghost tours around the town of Waukesha. Not only that, but Mike "had *his* own experience with a tall shadow man," according to Allison (Ibid.). You will learn a great deal more about Huberty's encounter—and other strange, Slenderman-themed issues—in a later chapter.

"IF ENOUGH PEOPLE BELIEVE SOMETHING IS TRUE, MAYBE IT IS"

A further Slenderman-based synchronicity can be found in the story of Tea Krulos. He is the author of a 2015 book called *Monster Hunters*, which is an eye-opening, entertaining, and

"It reminds me of A Nightmare on Elm Street." Wendy Schreier Photography.

witty look at people like me who spend their lives pursuing supernatural enigmas, such as Bigfoot, lake-monsters, UFOs, and more. Not only does Krulos have an interest in the Slenderman issue, but back in the early 2000s his parents moved to live in…Waukesha, Wisconsin. In fact, the attack on Payton Leutner occurred only a short distance from their home.

Krulos says: "Personally, I can say that it really upset my mom a lot. She was following the news, too. It was very shocking. There's crime in Waukesha, but nothing like that; certainly nothing like that. So, to have a small girl stabbed is pretty shocking. Most people in town were alarmed by it" (Redfern-Krulos, interview, 2017).

Krulos told me that this connection he had to the town, via his parents, "added a little bit of closeness to me, I guess." Indeed, it did; he followed the affair extensively. In 2017, Krulos said to me:

When the case happened it struck me as really intense because of the young age of the girls; it was terrible that this had happened. It happened pretty close to my parents' house. I never lived in Waukesha, but my parents moved to Waukesha about 15 years ago. And one of the themes I was working on in *Monster Hunters* is what's real and what's not. And how people interpret reality. So, I just became very curious in the [Geyser-Weier] case; I followed it in the local news. And, then, I actually went to their first trial date. I was just curious to witness it (Ibid.).

There was yet another synchronicity that revolved around the person sitting next to Krulos in the courtroom.

I got there and the courtroom was very crowded and they had actually sat me next to one of the girls' fathers; Morgan's father. That was an intense experience: When his daughter walked in the courtroom he began to cry quite a bit. It was so surreal to see this little girl, who was in a prison jumpsuit, which was probably the smallest they could find. It was baggy on her and she was in handcuffs. Shackles on her feet. It was heartbreaking to see that. So, I followed the case since…I went to the second trial date and followed the case through the media (Ibid.).

Krulos also checked out the area for himself.

A couple of days after the incident, I retraced the crime scene. Walking along Rivera Drive, I ran into three young girls, quietly carrying messages they had written on signboard. I approached them, and they told me they were classmates of the victim and were showing their support. "YOU AND YOUR FAMILY ARE IN OUR HEARTS! STAY STRONG, BELLA!" read one. The girls explained that Bella was the victim's nickname. "OUR HEARTS GO OUT TO THE VICTIM," read another sign, shaped like a Valentine heart. A pink teddy bear was placed next to it (Krulos, 2015).

Krulos, too, thinks the idea that the Slenderman may be some form of Tulpa is a valid and plausible one. He says of that particular theory:

Yes, I think this is very interesting. Something like a Tulpa; I think that's a very interesting theory. It ties in a lot with mythology and religion: If enough people believe something is true, maybe it is. I think the popularity is it's such a classic boogeyman; everyone likes a good story about the boogeyman. And add to that the viral nature of the Internet, it made it a popular thing. It's a classic creepy symbol: the sharp black suit. I think it ties in with a fear of authority a little bit (Redfern-Krulos, interview, 2017).

As we brought the interview to a close, Krulos said, reflecting on the location and the frenzied attack:

> Wisconsin in general has a weird and gruesome history. It's where Ed Gein was from and Jeffrey Dahmer. Waukesha is a very conservative place— middle-class and working class—but it reminds me of *A Nightmare on Elm Street*; a movie which, of course, had its very own infernal boogeyman in the form of Freddy Krueger (Ibid.).

A LABYRINTH FILLED WITH SYNCHRONICITIES

We now come to what is surely the most bizarre synchronicity in relation to the Slenderman. It all revolves around Guillermo Del Torro's acclaimed 2006 movie *Pan's Labyrinth*. It is a production that mixes extreme violence and enchanting fantasy in war-torn Spain in 1944. The movie tells of the short and tragic life of a young girl named Ofelia played by actress Ivana Baquero. The movie begins with Ofelia and her mother, Carmen, journeying to meet the ruthless Captain Vidal, who is destined to soon become Carmen's new husband and Ofelia's new father. It's the captain's job to seek out the many Republican rebels who are hunkered down in the deep woods that surround Vidal's camp.

It becomes very clear that Captain Vidal and Ofelia are not going to become friends. As a result, and amid the chaos, bloody violence, and death, Ofelia retreats further and further into a much grimmer and far more savage equivalent of *The Chronicles of Narnia*. We are never sure if Ofelia's other world is the real deal, or if she has descended into a state of mental illness and into a fantasy domain of her own making. Whatever the answer it's a world filled with all manner of magical entities: fairies, a mandrake in human form, a huge and deadly toad, and a faun; the latter being the "Pan" of the movie's title. As for the labyrinth, it's a magical, old structure in the woods where Ofelia finally meets her end; she is callously shot dead by Captain Vidal, who is then himself killed by the rebels. In the final moments of the movie, we are led to believe that Ofelia has reincarnated in the form of a long-dead princess named Moanna. Or, is it all the product of Ofelia's mind as she takes her final breaths and her brain shuts down forever? We're never really sure. Del Toro, though, has implied in interviews that Ofelia's dream world is no dream, after all.

Now, we come to the Slenderman connections.

WELCOME TO THE WORLD OF THE PALE MAN

One of the most terrifying characters in *Pan's Labyrinth* is a monstrous humanoid known as the "Pale Man." Like the Slenderman, the Pale Man is a mockery of a human. He is pretty much faceless; his eyes are set in the palms of his pale hands and he is hairless. Also like the Slenderman, who has a mansion in the woods, the Pale Man has his very own creepy lair in which he dwells. And he has a deranged taste for the flesh of young children. The parallels between the Slenderman and the Pale Man are as graphic as they are glaringly obvious.

Eric Knudsen has not stated, or even intimated, that the Pale Man was integral to his creation of the Slenderman. It must, however, be stressed that the slendermanconnection.wikia.com website states firmly that the Pale Man is "believed to be one of the inspirations" for the Slenderman. Given the fact that *Pan's Labyrinth* was released in 2006, it's not at all impossible that the Pale Man *may* have become a part of the development of the Slenderman three years later. But, there is one aspect of the story that could not have been anticipated back in 2009. Namely, how the ending of the movie parallels the events at Waukesha, which occurred eight years after the movie hit cinemas worldwide ("The Pale Man, *Pan's Labyrinth*," 2017).

In both cases, fact and fiction, we have young girls increasingly descending into a world of fantasy, but which may not be *just* fantasy. We have the Pale Man wreaking havoc and pursuing children in much the same way as the Slenderman does. The Pale Man even closely resembles the Slenderman. Or vice-versa. In Waukesha we have a girl who almost lost her life within the trees of David's Park, and in *Pan's Labyrinth* we have the main character, Ofelia, who is violently killed in a labyrinth surrounded by woods, but who may have been pulled back from the brink of death by reincarnation. And things get even weirder.

THE SYNCHRONICITIES CONTINUE

As noted, the star of 2006's *Pan's Labyrinth* was Ivana Baquero, who played Ofelia. Three years later, Baquero starred in Luis Berdejo's movie *The New Daughter*. Baquero's character Louisa James is the daughter of the movie's title. *The New Daughter* is a strange story, at the heart of which is a colony of ancient, primitive humanoid creatures that somewhat resemble the Pale Man of *Pan's Labyrinth* (the eyes aside) and who dwell deep in millennia-old mysterious mounds and tunnels. Just like Ofelia, Louisa dies at the end in violent fashion and in the woods.

Linda Godfrey, the author of such books as *Hunting the American Werewolf* and *Monsters Among Us*, notes that early explorers to the United States were amazed by the discovery of "staggeringly large numbers of precisely formed earth mounds that graced the landscape; some 20,000 or more in at least 3,000 locations." Aside from a number of such creations in Illinois, Minnesota, and Iowa, the vast majority of the mounds are found within the state of Wisconsin. Their purpose has been hotly debated for years. Linda Godfrey offers the most popular theories: burial mounds, tribal totem makers, and ceremonial centers (Godfrey, 2006).

In *Indian Mounds of Wisconsin*, Robert A. Birmingham and Leslie E. Eisenberg say "Three conical mounds preserved in Cutler Park are typical of those built during the Middle Woodland stage, approximately 2,000 years ago" (Birmingham, 2000).

It turns out that Cutler Park is situated less than two-and-a-half miles from David's Park, which is where Payton Leutner was stabbed.

And, finally, the actor who played the Pale Man in *Pan's Labyrinth*, Doug Jones, took on the role of the Operator in the earlier-mentioned Marble Hornets' movie, *Always Watching* in 2015. The Operator was, of course, the Slenderman in just about everything conceivably possible, except for the name.

8

"THERE WILL BE NO SAFETY IN THIS HOUSE"

nly a week after the horrific attack on Payton Leutner there was yet another violent knife assault that also had ties to the Slenderman phenomenon. And the attacker was, once again, a young girl. This time, the location was Hamilton County, Ohio. It was a story that the local media immediately picked up on, chiefly because the incident occurred in the immediate aftermath of the events at Waukesha, which had already received a massive amount of publicity. The story told by the 13-year-old girl's mother, who was given anonymity by law enforcement officers and the media, sounds like something straight out of a late-night horror movie. This was not fiction, however. Far from it.

Interviewed by WLWT News 5, the mother revealed that on the night in question, she came home from work on what, up until then, had been a perfectly normal day. There was nothing normal about what was to happen next, however. The mother walked into the kitchen only to be confronted by her daughter, who was wearing a hoodie and a deathly pale mask, and wielding a large, sharp knife. The daughter, her mother said, somewhat ominously, had been waiting for her. The girl then suddenly lunged forward and launched a full-on assault, cutting her mother's neck, slicing into her face, and inflicting a significant wound to her back.

An obsession with the Slenderman

It wasn't long before the emergency services were on the scene and the girl was placed in the Hamilton County Juvenile Detention Center—for the good of pretty much everyone, one might suggest. That was when the full and deeply disturbing truth of the affair came tumbling out. After the girl's mother was treated for the cuts and lacerations, she was interviewed by the police about the attack. It turns out this was not a domestic argument gone wild. It was far worse than that.

The mother told law enforcement officials that it was as if her daughter had become someone else during the attack, that she had certain psychological problems, and that she had an unhealthy obsession with the Slenderman, to the extent that she had written extensively about him in her journal and had drawn Slenderman-themed imagery in that same journal, too. Feeling that she was going mad, that demons were plaguing her, and that a mysterious darkness was going to envelop her, the girl was clearly in a deeply traumatized state. One didn't have to be an expert to realize that.

WLWT News 5's Karin Johnson was told by the mother:

> [My daughter] mentioned playing a role. It didn't feel like her at all. She was someone else during that attack. We found things that she had written and she made reference to Slenderman. She also made references to killing. She even created a world for Slenderman in the game Minecraft [a video game of the "Sandbox" variety] (Evans, 2014).

Techopedia describes such games as ones in which "Minimal character limitations are placed on the gamer, allowing the gamer to roam and change a virtual world at will…. Instead of featuring segmented areas or numbered levels, a sandbox game usually occurs in a 'world' to which the gamer has full access from start to finish" ("Sandbox, 2017).

Notably, the girl's mother came to believe that her daughter was "under the same influence" as that which took a decisive and unrelenting grip on Anissa Weier and

Morgan Geyser. Whether that "influence" was provoked by psychological conditions that plagued the minds of all three girls, or by something supernaturally slender in nature that had taken decisive strides out of the Internet and into our reality, still very much remains to be seen (Evans, 2014).

FANNING THE FLAMES

Just three months after the knife attack in Hamilton County, Ohio, yet *another* tragic and danger-filled event occurred. This time, it was in Pasco, Florida. Yet again, the one who caused so much chaos was a young girl—a 14-year-old girl, to be exact. Teenage years can be difficult at the very best of times; just about everyone can attest to that. But when one adds to that the terrifying Slenderman, it's very much like taking a match to a keg or several sticks of dynamite. In fact, that actually was not far from what really happened.

It was early September. The time? The dead of night. All was quiet on Pasco's Hermitage Lane. It was not destined to remain quiet, though. The girl in question was wide awake, filled with anger and frustration, after being told by her mother to do a bunch of chores earlier in the evening. As a result, she decided to take things out on her mother in a drastic and extreme fashion. She took a bathroom towel, soaked it in a dangerous and volatile cocktail of bleach and alcohol, and then set it alight in the garage.

Then, she fled the scene. Luckily, the girl's mother and her young son were woken up by the powerful smell of smoke and ran out of the house screaming. Mother and son were frantic; where was the girl, a daughter to one and a sister to the other? Little did they know that she had made her stealthy way to a rest room located in the confines of a nearby park. She had with her a number of knives and flashlights, as well as food and drink. Clearly, things had been planned as ruthlessly as they were carefully.

Firefighters were quickly on the scene; it took almost a dozen and a half of them to extinguish the roaring inferno. Thankfully, they were there just in time to prevent the rapidly escalating fire from spreading to surrounding homes, such as that of Jim Colucci, the immediate next-door neighbor, and someone who just managed to get his family and their pet dog to safety, as well as moving his car out of harm's way.

The girl, quickly regretting her actions, texted her mother saying that she was sorry for what she had done. The police were far from impressed by her poor attempt of what amounted to an apology. She was taken to the Pasco Juvenile Assessment Center and charged with arson and two counts of attempted murder. It was then that the Slenderman connection reared its (faceless) head. Like the girl who viciously stabbed her mother in June 2014 in Hamilton County, Ohio, this one too kept a journal. The words *Keep Out* dominated its front cover. And its pages, too, made references to the Internet's most threatening monster in a black suit. References to Anissa Weier and Morgan Geyser were contained in its pages, also. And, as what may have been a warning of the carnage that hit the family home, the girl had written in her journal: "If this keeps up there will be no safety in this house." The girl, the police soon learned, was also a fan of *CreepyPasta Wiki*, which, as we have seen, played an integral role in the early development of the Slenderman phenomenon (Moran, 2014).

Chris Nocco, Pasco's sheriff, confirmed to the media that the girl openly admitted to having started the fire. The local police were, however, seemingly surprised by her appearance. On several occasions the police made references to her not following "an extreme Gothic type of role" and stressed that she didn't "dress all in black." As an aside, it must be said that stereotyping those who find themselves drawn to the world of the Slenderman as nothing but black-wearing Goths is as unfair as it is wholly incorrect. History has shown that teenagers from all walks of life, and with varying tastes of fashion, have been ensnared by the supernatural thing. The Slenderman doesn't care a damn about your background. Nor does he care about your clothing or your lifestyle. All he wants to do is get his claws into you and his tentacles wrapped around you forever (Orlando, 2014).

Darkness in Dakota

There's absolutely no doubt that the most tragic and almost unbelievable Slenderman-themed deaths kicked off in late December 2014 and continued well into 2015. The location was the roughly 3,500 square-mile Pine Ridge Indian Reservation in South Dakota. It is the domain of the Oglala Lakota people, who are direct descendants of the Sioux. Between 2014 and 2015, close to a dozen young people, ranging in age from 12 to 24, and for whom the reservation was their home, committed suicide. More than *100* youngsters attempted suicide but failed. Very possibly, many were classic cries for help, rather than serious attempts to end lives. Sadly, suicide and teenagers often go together, hand in glove. But there was something else at work on the old, 19th-century reservation during that period when lives were lost and families were plunged into states of utter devastation; it was something both sinister and dangerous.

It's important to note that the reservation and its people are not without a few strikes against them. Alcohol abuse is rife, as is the misuse of both illegal and prescription drugs. Many of the people cannot find work. And the average lifespan for men of the Pine Ridge Indian Reservation is less than *50 years old*. I mention this to demonstrate that when faced with such conditions, cases of suicide might be expected. There is, however, another issue that cannot be ignored. You know what—or, rather, who—is coming.

SUICIDE AND A "MAN" NAMED SAM

The Native Americans of the Pine Ridge Indian Reservation believe in the existence of a dangerous and supernatural creature they refer to as the Tall Man Spirit. It is also known as Walking Sam, a name that has proven to be easily the most popular of the two monikers. He or it—take your pick—looks unsettlingly like the Slenderman. Walking Sam is in excess of seven feet in height and, just like the Slenderman, he doesn't have much in the way of meat on his bones. His arms and legs are long and spidery and he lacks a mouth. Peter Matthiessen, who in 1983 wrote a book about the area and its people titled *In the Spirit of Crazy Horse*, said that it is "both spirit and real being, but he can also glide through the forest, like a moose with big antlers, as though the trees weren't there" (Matthiessen, 1992).

Note that Matthiessen references Walking Sam in a forest-based context, which is the preferred domain of the Slenderman. And just like the Men in Black, the Shadow People, and the Mad Gasser of Mattoon—all of which were inspirations for Eric Knudsen's spindly beast in black—Walking Sam wears a black hat. In his case, though, it's usually of the old stovepipe variety. Walking Sam, like the Slenderman, is alleged to have the ability to take control of peoples' minds. We might accurately call it a form of mind-enslavement. Perhaps this might explain a deeply disturbing event that occurred on a particular day in February 2015.

A large number of teenagers from the Pine Ridge Indian Reservation headed out to a specific area of land that was dominated by trees. There was a notable reason for this, albeit hardly a positive one. The plan was for each one of them to hang themselves by the neck from the trees, which explained why they all went to the area armed with nothing but rope. Thankfully, John Two Bulls, a local pastor, heard of what was about to go down and quickly managed to stop what would very likely have become a mass suicide of almost unthinkable proportions. More than a few of the tribespeople were privately of the opinion that Walking Sam—not unlike the gruesome and insanely evil Pied Piper—had led the teenagers to what almost turned out to be their place of death.

This particular theory is bolstered by the words of a minister, Chris Carey, who works with the kids who live on the reservation. He says that the Tall Man Spirit/Walking Sam seems to be telling the young people on the reservation to take their lives. Intriguingly, the monster does so by inserting itself on the Internet, its shadowy, spindly form appearing on-screen, which is very similar to the 2016 experience of "Lacy," discussed in an earlier chapter. As we've seen, the Slenderman too is an entity that haunts the Internet—further evidence that Walking Sam and the Slenderman are very likely two parts of the very same phenomenon (Romano, 2015).

"Red Pill Junkie," a regular contributor to the popular website *Mysterious Universe* says that what we have here may amount to "…a cultural 'remix' between the older myth of the Tall Man/Suicide Spirit which already existed among Native Americans prior to the rise of the World Wide Web, and the newer, more potent icon of Slenderman introduced to these communities through the pervasiveness of new social networks…"

9

"DEMON-POSSESSED"

ertainly, the most tragic of all the Slenderman-linked attacks and deaths were those perpetrated on June 8th, 2014, by a crazed husband and wife. Their names were Jerad and Amanda Miller. It was in Las Vegas, Nevada, on the day in question that the deranged pair left a trail of death and bloody mayhem behind them. Their lives were over too, both at the hands of the local police. Notably, the Millers were heavily into cosplay and Jerad Miller was known to have a particular fascination for the Slenderman. He was also driven to dress like the Slenderman, too, even to the point of wearing an almost-faceless, white mask. Before we get to the matter of the killings, though, let's first take a look at the pair, their backgrounds, their motivations, and what it was exactly that led them on their insane path to murder.

Born in 1983, Jerad Miller was a street performer and someone with a distinctly long and checkered past with the world of law enforcement. He had run-ins with the police as far back as 2001, mostly for minor offenses. That situation would eventually change, however. Six years later, he pleaded guilty to a felony charge. Two years after that, Miller was hit with a charge of assault, although in this case he was very lucky to have walked free. Then, in 2011, Miller was up on a drugs charge. Yet again, it was a felony that saw Miller in front of a judge. This was the same year in which Miller and Amanda Woodruff, born in 1992, met and got married. It was on the 22nd of the month that the two wed in Lafayette, Indiana, living on the city's Weaver Street in a small apartment. Unlike Miller, Woodruff had no convictions of any kind at all. Under his spell and influence, however, her character was soon destined to change, and not for the better. The pair was not content with Lafayette; they were soon looking to make a significant move to a new town. And they did exactly that.

"DEMON-POSSESSED"

A BUILD-UP TO VIOLENCE IN VEGAS

In January 2014, the new home of the Millers became Sin City itself: Las Vegas. The Millers found an apartment located on Bruce Street at the Oak Tree Apartments. It wasn't long at all before the pair became the talk of the neighbors. Mostly, this was because of their liking of dressing up as superheroes and supervillains and parading around the apartments in their fantasy gear. Amanda had a thing for Harley Quinn, a super-villainess created by DC Comics back in 1992. For Jerad it was primarily the Slenderman and the Joker from the Batman comic books. (Both Batman and the Joker are the creations of DC Comics, too.) There was, however, something else: Jerad Miller didn't just dress like the Slenderman, he was also deeply interested in the whole Slenderman phenomenon. Yes, the macabre monster of the Internet had got its tentacles into yet another soul.

Neighbors occasionally saw the pair hitting the town on weekend nights with Amanda dressed in her red Harley garb and accompanying Harley pigtails, and Jerad in full-on Slenderman splendor. He had the black suit, the white shirt, the skinny black tie, and a pale, blank mask that displayed just two eye-holes and a slit for a mouth. One neighbor remarked that Jerad had once told him the pair had been asked to leave a local Vegas strip-club for being inappropriately dressed, which is kind of ironic, to say the very least. They had a swinging private life and occasionally held costume parties, at which everyone was expected to dress for the occasions (which included coming as the Slenderman, so to speak). Of course, there's nothing at all wrong with having a bit (or even a lot) of fun on a weekend night or two. For the Millers, however, what was perceived by some of their neighbors as just a bit of alternative behavior would eventually mutate into something just about as dark as dark could be.

Although the cosplay (with weekend benefits…) continued at a steady pace, a change began to slowly develop in Jerad Miller. It was far from being a positive change; it oozed negativity. That change involved Miller not exactly giving up his supervillain costumes, but adding to them. The primary addition collectively amounted to a collection of military-style camouflage-type clothing, gloves, and black combat boots. A good sign, this most certainly was not. Miller then chose to up the ante to just about the highest level possible when he started posting anti-police comments, rants, and links on multiple forms of social media, usually when he was dressed up as the Joker, complete with the character's famous iconic make-up. Miller also had nothing good to say about the ever-increasing state of surveillance that we now live in. His fury and frustration at the world around him, and particularly at elements of the U.S. government, were growing as quickly as his mind was seething and whirling. He encouraged nation-wide revolution and, incredibly and outrageously, was of the opinion that the victims of the 1999 Columbine High School killings in Colorado got what they deserved. Miller was, by now, a ticking time bomb of the most dangerous type conceivable. And the countdown to destruction was getting ever closer.

Amanda Miller, by now completely under the sway of her deranged and dangerous husband, dutifully followed suit, making Facebook posts that suggested she just might go on a shooting spree, which is exactly what did happen, with her husband orchestrating the entire situation. It was only a matter of time before the Millers were destined to become prime-time, national news, but for all of the wrong reasons. They were about to be two of the most hated and despised people in the entire country. Lives were about to end. And families were soon in states of hysteria and mourning.

Murder and a stand-off at Walmart

The deadly affair all began late on the morning of June 8, 2014, when the Millers made their way to a pizza eatery in Las Vegas. Incredibly, they made the walk on foot. I say "incredibly" because the pair was packing significant fire-power at the time and not a single soul noticed.

The two marched into the restaurant and headed straight for their intended targets, who happened to be a pair of police officers, Alyn Beck and Igor Soldo, having their lunch after a morning of work. Jerad Miller wasted no time putting his plan into action and he callously shot officer Soldo in the back of the head, killing him immediately. Beck was shot in the throat, but he did not die instantly. In fact, he valiantly fought back against the rapidly growing odds. It was, however, all to no avail; in seconds, and after a volley of shots, officer Beck was dead, too. Before leaving, the Millers grabbed both officers' guns, extra bullets, and even their badges, too. If that was not enough, they then hauled the bodies of the two men out of the booth and onto the floor and shrouded them with a flag that had a swastika prominently adorned on it. The rest of the fear-filled customers could only look on in terror and horror.

On exiting the restaurant, the Millers then quickly headed off to a local Walmart. Those in the store were soon in a state of chaos; the duo entered the store, fired a bunch of bullets into the ceiling, and told everyone to leave. One brave soul tried to stop them, but he was destined to immediately pay with his life. The man was 31-year-old Joseph Robert Wilcox, also of Las Vegas. Unknown to anyone but Wilcox, he had a gun on him. When Wilcox realized what was going on, he challenged Jerad Miller, pointing his gun directly at Miller. It could have ended up as a stand-off with no one killed. That is, if it were it not for one terrible thing, something that Wilcox didn't anticipate and simply could not have foreseen. When he pulled out his weapon and had Jerad Miller solidly in his sights, Wilcox didn't realize that Miller had an accomplice, namely his wife, Amanda Miller. Wilcox assumed she was another customer, just like him. How tragically wrong Wilcox was. As he passed by Amanda Miller to confront her husband, Amanda Miller quickly stepped in and fatally shot Wilcox. He fell to the floor, victim number three of the crazed pair.

To their credit, the police were quickly on the scene. The pair retreated to one of the furthest parts of the store, seeking cover and looking to see what their options were. While contemplating, Jerad Miller was hit by a salvo of bullets and was quickly dead. As for Amanda Miller, she was hit in the head. She was rushed to a local hospital, but didn't last long; the bullet did exactly what it was supposed to do. It was a very good thing that the deranged two were taken out of circulation permanently: When police checked their backpacks, they found hundreds of rounds of ammunition and a shotgun. And a later, subsequent search of their home revealed a large amount of nutty, white supremacist material in their possession. Clearly, the two could have taken many more lives had they not been cut down in the Walmart. But even three was three too many.

THE GAME OF THE NAME

When the story broke, most people quite naturally assumed that the deaths of officers Alyn Beck and Igor Soldo, and of Joseph Robert Wilcox too, were simply the result of deranged actions from a pair of maniacs who had crossed the line from being fans of fantasy-fiction to outright assassins. That may well have been the case. But *most* people are not *all* people. Historian Michael Hoffman said:

> Whatever the Las Vegas killers' political affiliation may be…these suicide shooters, like James Holmes [of the 2012 Aurora, Colorado shootings], are first and foremost demon-possessed. These murderers worship Satan, whether under that name, or as "Joker" or "Slender Man." The people they kill are a propitiation to the god of this world.

Then, there is the matter of where the Millers got married: the city of Lafayette, Indiana. It brings us to what Loren Coleman of the *Twilight Language* blog calls "The Fayette Factor." He explains: "A surprisingly high incidence of Fortean (inexplicable) events linked to places named after one of the USA's Founding Fathers—the Marquis de Lafayette," a major, historical figure in the War of Independence, which ran from 1775 to 1783.

Encounters with ghosts, the clandestine activities of secret societies, controversial and complex conspiracy theories, and even sightings of Bigfoot creatures are linked to places named Lafayette in the United States to a much greater degree than towns and hamlets of other names. As Tony "Doc" Shiels—both a Chaos Magician and a "surrealchemist"—calls it, "the game of the name," a curious phenomenon for which "Lafayette" is a perfect example (Downes, 2006).

And, of course, there is the significant fact that Jerad Miller had an obsession with the Slenderman, even to the point that he would dress like the monster itself. The game of the name, the theoretical demonic angle of the Millers' killings, and the influence of the Slenderman are all indicative of a possibility that the tragic series of Las Vegas killings on June 8, 2014, may have had "outside influences," perhaps influences of none other than a supernatural and slender sort.

10

"EVIL LIES IN WAIT FOR AN EXCUSE TO BLOOM"

Of the many and varied people who have studied and investigated the Slenderman controversy, certainly one of the most learned is Jenny White Coleman, the wife of acclaimed cryptozoologist and Bigfoot authority Loren Coleman. Together, they run the International Cryptozoology Museum in Portland, Maine. In August 2014, Jenny Coleman's important article on the Slenderman, titled "Shadows of the Thin Man," was published in *Fortean Times* magazine. It provides the reader with valuable insight into the nature of the Slenderman and the phenomenon as a whole. In a June 2017 interview, I asked Coleman what it was that led her to immerse herself in the subject and what her thoughts on the creature are today. She told me:

> Honestly, Slenderman freaks me out. It's not a subject I enjoy, but one that has instead become "attached" to me. Loren, back in 2014, advised me to write the *FT* article based upon the interest surrounding the girls' stabbing attack of their friend; they of course committed the crime in order to "honor" Slenderman and earn a spot in his forest castle. Now, I do enjoy true crime documentaries, books, and articles; especially if there is a fantastic element, and this case ticked all the boxes. However, I do feel Slenderman itself is pure evil (Redfern-Coleman, interview, 2017).

In her article, Coleman said that the Slenderman is the "reborn face of an ancient evil." I asked her to explain what she meant by that. Jenny explains:

> In our current, Internet-, Smartphone-, iPad-obsessed culture, where people—especially young people—rarely look up from their screens, Slenderman is the opportunistic face, or mask, if you will, that evil has adopted. By "ancient evil," I mean supernatural evil. But, there are people who do not share my beliefs, and therefore this can be interpreted as

"the worst of mankind." Either way, I feel the terms "the Devil," "the Boogeyman," "demons," etc., are synonymous with Slenderman. It just happens that Slenderman has taken over the Internet, and therefore those obsessed with the Internet are most familiar with it. I also feel that people enjoy a sense of escapism with online horror stories such as those on *Creepypasta*. Maybe this escapism is tinged with the backlash against our current, political hypercorrectness; perhaps it is a way of dealing with the actual horrors of the real world. Who knows? (Ibid.).

"THERE'S SOMETHING DEEPLY DISTURBING ABOUT A BLANK WHITE FACE"

On the issue of why the Slenderman has created such phenomenal, massive interest, which clearly borders upon obsession on the part of many people, Jenny Coleman provides the following:

I think people have more *access* to the types of stories and information—in this case, creepy, evil, dark—in which they are interested. There are also the considerations of peer pressure, herd mentality, and "wanting to fit in" among the younger set. I also think the *appearance* of Slenderman strikes a chord. A primitive one. In my article, I talk about ophidiophobia [the fear of snakes], and I think this is highly relevant. Snakey arms, bald and pale, slimy, creepy, yucky: There is a reason this sort of appearance has been rife in scary stories and films throughout history. The *FT* article touches on much of that, but I would refer you as well to such films and books as *The Descent* and *Harry Potter* (Voldemort), and art (*The Scream*). And, actually, the movie *Scream* as well.

There's something deeply disturbing about a blank white face appearing from the darkness with intent to harm. Even *The Exorcist* uses that imagery. In summary, I believe that we, in our first-world comfort and freedom, with our access to all the awfulness of the world and all the freedom to poke and explore the gross parts of our brains, have found a sort of effigy in Slenderman. He represents all we are not and don't want to be…we hope (Ibid.).

Jenny Coleman has no doubt that the Slenderman imagery is nothing new, nor are encounters with the entity, even though it was not "officially" created until 2009:

"The Tall Man" and reports thereof have been around since early Irish and German mythology found a place in art and written word: *Fear Dubh* and *Der Grossman*, respectively. I would go so far as to say the Bible is *full* of these stories; wherever Satan is mentioned. Again, the snake. You can find ancient cave drawings reminiscent of the bald and pale and tall. There are *so many* different interpretations of Slenderman that it's almost impossible to funnel it into a definitive explanation. There are multiple comparisons of Slenderman with Indrid Cold [a creepy, endlessly grinning character who appears in John Keel's acclaimed 1975 book, *The Mothman Prophecies*]. Essentially, any creepy shadow-dweller is worthy of comparison. Jack the Ripper? Perhaps. Why not? This begs the question, if indeed the comparison with Cold and MIB is to be considered: Are "we" as a modern culture being "led" into these interests? Is there a greater scheme at play? (Ibid.).

That question is one we should all be concerned about. Perhaps the agenda of the Slenderman is so complex and massive that we fail to see the full picture.

"PEOPLE ARE ABSOLUTELY CAPABLE OF MANIFESTATION"

My next question for Jenny Coleman was: "To what extent, if at all, do you think the issue of the black suit—as a sign of authority—plays into all this?" She gave me the following:

I am not entirely sure that the black suit is a sign of "authority," although it may be. If, indeed, the MIB influence is as strong as some think, then yes, I would say it plays a huge role. However, it is my opinion that it's just the idea of the blank, white face looming out of the darkness that bites people in the primitive fear part of the brain (Ibid.).

Jenny makes a to-the-point comment on the Tulpa angle of the Slenderman affair: "I think this is highly, highly, strongly, one hundred percent valid. People are absolutely capable of manifestation. Evil lies in wait for an excuse to bloom and lure people to its fetid swamp-castle." Interestingly, Jenny suspects that both the Shadow People and the Black-Eyed Children fall into this particular category, too (Ibid.).

We then turned our attentions to the May 31, 2014, attempted murder of Payton Leutner by Morgan Geyser and Anissa Weier. Jenny's observations make for notable reading:

> I think two outcast little girls with highly fertile imaginations were allowed to screw around unbidden on the Internet. When we were kids, OMG, we dreamed up imaginary rooms at my Gram's house, and had places in the Maine woods that were absolutely magical and full of wonder. Trees in winter were walls of diamonds. We didn't even have access to cable television back then, and the world was

different. I'm not sure if the world was "less" evil, which I doubt, or if we just didn't know about how awful things could be. Kids are less innocent now. They just *are*. But with that lessened innocence comes an increased knowledge. And that can be—and was—a recipe for disaster (Ibid.).

I will leave you with the following words of Jenny Coleman, which amount to important observations on the overall issue: "Slenderman is just the modern face of ancient evil; it seems to be what people are focusing on now, especially after the boost it was given with the 2014 stabbings" (Ibid.).

11

"SLENDERMAN IS A PHYSICAL MANIFESTATION OF OUR FEAR OF DEATH"

O f the various people who have researched the Slenderman phenomenon, certainly one of the most visible is a
pastor named Robin Swope, who I interviewed in 2017
and who is the author of a book titled *Slenderman:
From Fiction to Fact*. Swope says of his background in
the church and his work in the field of the supernatural:

> I have a BA in biblical literature from Nyack
> College, which is an accredited biblical college of the
> Christian Ministry Alliance, in New York. And I have
> a Master of Divinity from the same denomination. I

was interested in stories of monsters when I was a kid, and drawn to cryptids—like Bigfoot—and UFOs and always wanted to have an experience. But, I never did. Until I had a faith crisis when I was 21. When I went into college that was when things started happening. I was witness to the Hudson River, New York, UFO flap in the mid-80s; I saw a huge, triangular-shaped UFO. I got involved with exorcisms, and a lot of experiences with things like supernatural entities.

The college that I went to, it used to be a tantric-sex country-club; I guess you can call it a country-club. They had all kinds of weird rituals and incantations going on there. When the Bible College got a hold of it, they exorcised every room, but strange things would still appear there. One room specifically had a mirror on the wall; it was kind of an artistic thing. But, dark faces kept appearing in the mirror. Beds moved and shook. Me and a friend had felt it and we saw in the mirror a shadow creature—the Shadow People. This was in 1987. We ran away, screaming. And we came back with a bunch of guys to pray. I always wondered what this was. We saw it, though (Redfern-Swope, interview, 2017).

"AN OVER-ARCHING ARCHETYPE"

As for how Pastor Swope became involved in the Slenderman controversy, he explains:

> A friend of mine, David Von Bostaph Bostash, told me about it; this was just within months of it being created in 2009. And then, I started reading about it. David is a local horror film critic who was VP of Horrorfest at the time and he pointed me to 4chan. At the time, 4chan, as well as other imageboards, were flooded with the Slenderman mythos, stories of encounters, and mish-mash histories and such. From 2009 to 2011, it was a constant flow. So, I started researching Slenderman and wrote a brief article on my blog. The response was incredible (Ibid.).

As a result of that phenomenal response, a book followed.

Still on the issue of the 2009 time frame, Swope firmly believes that when Eric Knudsen birthed the Slenderman, "He subconsciously tapped into an overarching archetype that was *already* there." This all very much ties in with the fact that, as will soon become apparent, we have numerous cases on file in which the Slenderman was seen long *before* 2009, as Swope's dossiers demonstrate—and as do other file-collections, too. The saga of how there may have been a Slenderman long before there was a Slenderman is a tale of incredible proportions and which will be expanded on in the next few chapters (Ibid.).

Fingers that grew and grew

One of the most fascinating cases that caught the attention of Swope came from a woman named Stacie Bogart, who Swope met with in 2011. She had a fascinating story to relate, a story that had both Slenderman- and Men in Black–themed overtones attached to it. Swope said to me that after he discussed the Slenderman phenomenon with Bogart, "When I was working at one of the local UPMC [University of Pittsburgh Medical Center] hospitals here in the region," she was somewhat shocked and amazed by Swope's description of the Slenderman, that she had heard a very similar story close to a decade earlier (Ibid.).

As Swope listened, Bogart explained how, back in 2002, she got to know a woman who had multiple supernatural encounters of the "alien abduction" kind, a woman whose story adds significant food for thought to the controversy surrounding the Slenderman.

Back in 1995, in the early hours of one particular morning, the woman had a traumatic encounter upon being woken from a deep sleep. All was certainly not well. There was something in the room; something that was clearly dangerous and threatening. It stood at the foot of the bed, menacingly, staring intently at the terrified woman. Swope says of the entity that it "was just like a Man in Black." That is, it was wearing the ubiquitous black suit and an old-style fedora hat. It was also very tall and extremely thin. How many times have we heard that? Even more familiar, Swope revealed to me that the

Robin Swope says that "Slenderman feeds on emotion." *Nick Redfern, 2016.*

creature stretched out its arms in the woman's direction. Suddenly, something even more horrifying happened: The bony fingers of the thing in black began to stretch…and stretch…and stretch. "Tendril fingers," as it was worded, proceeded to wrap around the woman's head. Not surprisingly, she quickly passed out. On regaining conscious, the woman was beyond relieved that the thing was now nowhere to be seen (Ibid.).

As a quick aside, it's worth noting that the issue of the creature having what were described as "tendril fingers" sounds very much like the tentacled fingers described in a 1953 case in Los Angeles, California, related by writer Harold T. Wilkins, as we saw earlier (Ibid.).

On the matter of this issue of the Slenderman stretching out its arms—in what is most assuredly never a welcoming fashion—Swope notes something intriguing from his body of research. He explained to me:

> I have noticed that when people see the creature in nature, like woods and forests, he has the tentacles. But in houses, he usually doesn't have them. In their homes, they see the arms reaching out, *stretching* out, almost like "Mr. Fantastic" in [Marvel Comics'] *The Fantastic Four*. But, there are no extraneous appendages coming from the body, except for when they are outside in the woods (Ibid.).

Certainly, this "stretching out" issue was an integral part of the 1995 case referenced above. And, it's also a case that demonstrates perfectly that the Slenderman was seen before its "official creation" in 2009.

From Slenderman to Slendermen

Robin Swope revealed to me another equally strange story; it's a story of not just one Slenderman, but an entire army of them. Again, it pre-dates 2009:

When I first started researching the phenomenon, I got a bunch of letters from pastors. One pastor from Ohio said that one day he was out in his field (he owned a farm) and by a forest edge, all of a sudden everything got quiet and it was twilight and a group of these creatures walked through the field. He had never told anybody; he just told me privately. Such an odd story (Ibid.).

"Odd" is arguably an understatement, as you will now see.

Swope's source wrote to him of the affair, which occurred back in the 1950s: "I glanced out the garage window and saw an entire line of these 'Slender People' coming out of the woods just beyond our neighbor's house. They were heading our way" (Ibid.).

The pastor added: "I was momentarily frozen," which is hardly surprising.

Notably, he added that: "They were all slender, but some were taller than others…. There were a few Slenders of small stature, whom I took to be children," all of whom were holding the hands of the taller ones. The pastor watched, filled with fear, as the skinny procession in black passed the property at a "slow, relentless pace," and finally vanished from sight. They did not return, which was surely a good thing from the perspective of the pastor (Ibid.).

A third case (of many) to reach Swope came from JoAnne, who, in August 2009 wrote:

From childhood I have seen this demonic figure. He is a tall shadow. He has no face, but he has long arms. Out of the corner of my eye on certain nights I see him and his arms seem to be reaching out to me, and when I turn to look at him, the thing is gone. I have the real feeling that if I don't turn around to look at him his arms will catch me up and I will die (Ibid.).

"HE'LL ALWAYS BE IN THE PERIPHERY"

Moving on from his case files, I asked Swope for his opinions on why, exactly, so many of the people who are attracted to, and adversely affected by, the Slenderman are young children and teenagers. His reply was one to muse upon, to be sure:

A lot of it *does* tie into the boogeyman archetype, where the whole thing is terrifying, at least for children. The whole mythos relies on the boogeyman. If you're bad, he's going to come and get you and take you away. With Slenderman, there's the fear of capture, fear that the arms will get you. That's why the arms are always long, or why there are extraneous limbs, tendrils (Ibid.).

In my book I summarize Slenderman as an overarching archetype of death. Slenderman, in the mythos, when you see him, he's going to haunt you. He'll always be in the periphery, waiting and wanting to get you and take you away—and that's what death is. I think that the boogeyman archetype is genetically in our make-up; because it has been there so long. So, I think it's a sub-context in the Id. I think that's the key to understanding Slenderman.

But, it's not just children and teenagers. Adults are affected, too. But, most of those who are affected—of *any* age—are very emotional. I think Slenderman feeds on emotion. And being a teenager is an emotional time. He specifically manifests on fear because it's the strongest emotion. It controls us, physically, in so many different ways. Through glands excreting hormones and through our nervous-system. Slenderman feeds on that and it helps him manifest. Part of it *might* be Tulpas, but, I think there's something *already* there that wants to *be* manifest, something that feeds on our fear (Ibid.).

"WE ARE SLENDERMAN'S PURPOSE"

Is the Slenderman phenomenon destined to continue, to grow, and to provoke more suicides, more attempted murders, and greater, terrible tragedy? Swope offers these words, which may not be particularly encouraging for those who have encountered the Slenderman up close and personal: "I think it's going to be a constant. Whenever humanity's in the mix, I think these things—like Slenderman, the Shadow People, the Men in Black—are going to be in the mix, too. And, I don't think that's going to change" (Ibid.).

If, then, the Slenderman *is* now destined to be with us forever—and, perhaps, in an ever-increasing fashion—can it be stopped? Are their ways and means that might help us to at least try and combat the dark and disturbing thing and dispatch it back to wherever it came from? Swope thinks it's not at all hopeless; there is some light at the end of the tunnel. From the perspective of his position as a pastor, he says:

> You can go the exorcising way, or the cleansing way, but what it really all comes down to is faith. And willpower. And, for whatever religion that might be. We are Slenderman's purpose. He may even be a *part* of us. If you look at the word "demon," and how it evolved over the centuries, the first time we see that meaning in Homer's epics, it's just a soul; it's nothing else. But by the time the Neoplatonic philosophers got to it, you have the angel on one side and the demon on the other. But it's really describing *us.* That we have a good part and a bad part. And they both manifest in the world. The bad part, as the ancients saw it, is in us and outside of us. And that's the same with us: *We* are manifesting Slenderman. So, because we are manifesting it,

we *can* make it go away. Clinging onto faith and the good and to commanding it to go away. That's why I believe prayer is an active, powerful weapon—of *any* faith. The way is willpower and hope and faith (Ibid.).

Swope's final words to me on the matter of the world's most ominous monster: "Whether it's a Tulpa, demonic, or something else, Slenderman is a physical manifestation of our fear of death" (Ibid.).

12

"AND IN DID COME THE STRANGEST FIGURE"

The Slenderman is perceived by many—even those who faithfully follow just about each and every development in the controversy—as a creature that surfaced specifically in the summer of 2009 at *Something Awful*. That is not *entirely* correct, though. In fact, some might argue it is way off the mark. There are numerous examples of cases and incidents that have distinct Slenderman-themed overtones attached to them, but in some cases they are decades old (and, in other cases, even *centuries* old). *He* may have been among us for much longer than we can possibly imagine or conceive.

As noted in Chapter 11, Robin Swope suggested an intriguing theory for how there could have been a Slenderman in the past when it was not created until the 21st century. He suspects that Eric Knudsen "subconsciously tapped into an overarching archetype that was *already* there." The cases that follow in the next few chapters certainly suggest that Swope is on the right track (Redfern-Swope, interview, 2017).

We will begin with the famous saga of the Pied Piper of Hamelin. It's seen by most people as a story designed to entertain children, which in many respects it is. It's a fact, though, that as well as being engrossing, it's a decidedly disturbing tale, too. Just like the Slenderman of today, the Pied Piper of yesteryear was someone who had a supernatural influence over children and who would steal them away to his magical abode. Not a particularly warming tale. Yes, the comparisons are already there. And, as you'll soon see, the list of unhealthy comparisons only continues to grow.

The saga of the Pied Piper dates back to the latter part of the 13th century. As for the location, Hamelin, it's a town that stands on the River Weser in Germany's Lower Saxony region and one that has a history dating back to the ninth century, more than a thousand years ago. What we know for sure is that the first reference to the story of the Pied Piper of Hamelin came not from the pages of an ancient book or a faded old manuscript, but from a piece of stained-glass window in the town's local place of worship—a church that was demolished midway through the 17th century. So, the window is long gone, but the talk of it most certainly endures.

So the story goes, at some point in the late 1200s, the people of Hamelin found themselves under what can only be termed as a state of siege, but not by hostile neighbors or by invading armies. Hamelin had been overrun by rats—thousands of them. Maybe even tens of thousands of the creatures. The townsfolk had no clue how to bring the massive wave of rats to an end. But, *someone* knew. At the height of the infestation, a mysterious and oddly dressed character wandered into town. It was, of course, that strange and enigmatic Pied Piper—"Pied" meaning decorated—which is a reference to the man's multi-colored, almost clown-like, garb.

The new figure in town had a decidedly alternative way of ridding Hamelin of its ever-growing body of rats. There was not a bit of rat poison in sight. Not a single weapon was in evidence. So, how was the man going to make good on his promise to end the problem? The only thing the Pied Piper had with him was a pipe (hence the title he became famously known by), which he would play in the same fashion that someone would play a flute. The Pied Piper had a unique way of getting rid of the pesky rats. By playing an enchanting and hypnotic tune, the Piper assured the mayor of Hamelin, he could lure the entire rat population into the waters of the River Weser. Each and every one of them would quickly meet their end by drowning. The townsfolk, after being inundated with rats for far too long, were more than willing to give just about anything a try. In return, the Piper asked for a payment of 1,000 guilders (in English terminology, "golden pennies"). The mayor eagerly agreed to the payment and a deal was struck. (A deal of the Faustian type? You bet.)

The Pied Piper stuck to the terms of the deal and he placed the pipe to his lips. Near-mesmerizing music began to echo eerily around the town; it caused the rats to stop whatever they were doing and follow the Piper as he made his way to the banks of the River Weser. (It must have been a daunting, and even disturbing, sight to see thousands and thousands of rats marching to their deaths behind the mysterious Piper.) In no time at all, the rats were dead, drowned in the deep waters of the old river. Admittedly, in some versions of the story, one of the rats managed to survive and fled the town, which was probably a very wise decision on its part. It should have been a time for celebration, except for one thing: The mayor of Hamelin quickly went back on his promise to fill the Piper's pockets with gold. In an effort to try and justify his actions, the mayor accused the Piper of deliberately bringing the rats to Hamelin as a means to then try and bleed the town dry of its money. True or not, the Pied Piper warned the mayor that Hamelin had not seen the last of him and he added that terrible things were about to befall its people. This was no idle threat on the part of the Piper. He angrily strode out of town, but it wasn't long before he was back. It was time for revenge of the most cold-hearted type possible.

HAMELIN'S CHILDREN GO AWOL

The 15th-century Luneberg Manuscript, the oldest known written account of the Pied Piper's presence in Hamelin, states that on June 26th, 1284, a day celebrating the lives of the saints John and Paul, 130 children vanished under mysterious circumstances. How could such a thing have happened? And why did the townsfolk not try and stop it from happening in the first place? Given the fact that the day in question was a deeply religious one, all of the adults had congregated in the church to celebrate the lives of the two famous saints, the aforementioned John and Paul. The children, meanwhile, were outside playing in the streets. *All* of them. As fate would have it, this would prove to be their downfall.

The tale continues that as he strode back into town the Pied Piper pulled out his pipe and began to play an entrancing tune. It was so entrancing that it encouraged all of the children to follow the Piper as he turned on his heels and headed for the hills. In almost slave-like and zombified fashion, the children unquestioningly followed the mysterious man whose music could control minds.

Of course, the big question is this: How do we know for sure that all of the children *were* taken away by the Pied Piper considering all of the adults were in the church at the time of the mass disappearance? Who was left to reveal what happened to them? Reportedly, there were three children who were lucky enough not to have fallen victim to the Piper's terrible tunes. One was deaf, and so was obviously not affected by the strange music. Another was blind and fell behind the line of children and, as a result, was lucky enough not to fall into the Piper's clutches. And a third had a medical condition that affected the child's legs, preventing him from keeping up with the rest of the group and, in effect, saving him from a life with the Pied Piper. It was only when the church celebrations were over, and the congregation spilled out onto the streets, that they realized something which provoked immediate hysteria from the parents: Aside from that lucky trio, Hamelin's children were no more. They were all gone, vanished with that mysterious player of the pipe. Chaos broke out as frantic mothers and fathers sought to find their missing children.

In Robert Browning's 1842 telling of the story of the Pied Piper of Hamelin, we're told that the two surviving children who could see revealed the following: "When, lo! as they reached the mountain-side, A wondrous portal opened wide, As if a cavern was suddenly hollowed; And the Piper advanced and the children followed, And when all were in to the very last, The door in the mountain-side shut fast" (Browning, 1842).

Hypnotizing the children: the Pied Piper of Hamelin. *Wikimedia Commons, 1888.*

Many might suggest that the story of the Pied Piper and the vanishing children is simply an old folkloric take, a tale designed to either entertain or terrify young children. But the fact that so many versions and variations exist is a good indication that there is at least some degree of truth to the story. Suggestions have been made that the children all died from a plague, perhaps a form of plague carried and spread by that overwhelming number of rats that invaded Hamelin in the final years of the 13th century. Maybe that's how the story came to have those two components—

children and rats—attached to it. Certainly, it's a theory that makes some sense. Problematic, though, is the fact that in some versions of the story the rats are completely absent and it's just the children who fall under the lure of the Piper's music. The possibility also exists that the Piper was really a pedophile—someone who callously and deliberately targeted the children one by one and lured them to isolated locales, such as the mountain to which Robert Browning referred.

In another telling of the tale, the Pied Piper agrees to return the children unharmed after the mayor of the town finally promises to pay the full amount for ridding Hamelin of its rats—and he *does* pay it. In that sense, the story has a happy ending, which is appropriate for a typical fairy tale. But we should not forget that this is just one of many variations on the old tale.

And, then, we have the Slenderman links to the controversy.

"TALL AND THIN" AND A KIDNAPPER OF CHILDREN

When we go back to Robert Browning's version of the story we're told (specifically when the Pied Piper first arrives in town) that: "And in did come the strangest figure: His queer long coat from heel to head Was half of yellow and half of red; *And he himself was tall and thin* [author's italics]" (Browning, 1842).

So, what we have here in the old tales is a man—"the strangest figure," which suggests there was something unusual about his appearance—who was both of significant height and skinny. He was also a man who had the mysterious ability to take control of the minds of children, even entire groups of them. The piper even seemed to have a disturbingly dark affinity with children, who would follow him without question, which is also extremely Slenderman-like. His followers and proxies will do just anything for him, as we saw with Anissa Weier and Morgan Geyser. Also very much like the Slenderman, the Piper dwelled in a magical realm, one to which he would take the children. In 13th-century Germany it was described as a "cavern" that was accessible by a "wondrous portal." Today, the Slenderman lures children to his mysterious, old mansion in the woods.

Might there have been an early incarnation of the Slenderman in Germany, circa the latter part of the 13th century? Was the presence of just such a Slenderman, and its large-scale kidnapping of huge numbers of children, something that led to the legend of the brightly clothed Pied Piper? These are questions that are not only unanswered, they are also questions that will probably never be answered to the satisfaction of everyone. All we can say with certainty is that when we go looking for pre-2009 reports of Slenderman-type entities and stories, we most certainly find them, even if they don't go by the specific name of the Slenderman.

Other such cases await, one of which involves the death of a child and the presence of a skinny figure in black. It's now time to take a trip back to Waukesha, Wisconsin, the site of the May 31, 2014 attack. What we will now see is that when it comes to Waukesha and the Slenderman, things did *not* begin with that savage assault on Payton Leutner. The history of Waukesha tells of very similar incidents that occurred years ago. Waukesha's history also shows that the city has been linked to the Slenderman for decades. In fact, close to a century. The Pied Piper, as a proto-Slenderman, is certainly not alone when it comes to the matter of early incarnations of one of the most dangerous supernatural creatures of all time.

13

"A SLIM MAN IN A DARK SUIT"

ike Huberty is the founder of the Waukesha Ghost Tour and the cohost of the "See You on the Other Side" podcast. He's also the sister of Allison Jornlin, who we met in Chapter 7 regarding the Slenderman-*Coast to Coast AM* controversy of May 31, 2014. In light of his work in the field of the paranormal and ghost-hunting, it's hardly surprising that when the 2014 Slenderman-driven stabbing in Waukesha occurred, Huberty took close notice of what took place. He could, after all, hardly miss it. Not only did he and Allison grow up in a *very* nearby town called Big Bend, but, back in the early 1990s, Huberty had what can only be described as a way-too-close-for-comfort encounter with a tall, shadowy figure of supernatural proportions, and only a handful of miles from where Payton Leutner almost lost her life years later. But that's not all.

Over the years, Huberty, who now lives in Madison, Wisconsin, has collected and investigated more than a few reports of strange and menacing entities in the Waukesha area. They include what have become known as the Water Man and the Smiley-Faced Man. Not only that, Huberty has also uncovered evidence of other violent attacks on children in the area, some with distinct paranormal and Slenderman-themed overtones attached to them. We'll begin exactly where we should: with Huberty's very own encounter of the tall, dark, and undeniably menacing type.

"THE SHADOW THING WOULD NOT REFLECT LIGHT"

One summer evening in 1993, me and a few friends had been over at another friend's house and he was talking about how he really wanted us to go see this evil-looking tree in what's known as Vernon Marsh [located in eastern Waukesha County, it's official title is the Vernon Wildlife Area]. We were just laughing about it. We said, kind of joking, "Okay, let's go and check out the evil-looking tree." It was me, two guys, and two girls. My friend said it was something demonic; he said he saw the hand of a demon burned into a tree. So, we got into the marshes—it was a bright night, a bright moon. And his house is maybe half a mile from where he says the tree is. But, it's into the marsh we have to go to find it. There are paths there, and signs, because there are hunters. This is all public land. We go in and we see the tree. And it's so super lame. There's nothing to it and we all laughed about it. I don't get a weird feeling from the tree; *nobody* gets a weird feeling from it. So, I'm kind of making fun of it; we all were.

We keep going further into the Vernon Marsh. I'm walking ahead with the two girls, and the two guys are behind us; maybe 20 yards. And we were just talking and we get close to a point in the pass where I see a sign—regulations telling you when you can hunt. It tells you when you *can* be there, and when you're *not* supposed to be there. And, at that time, we were *not* supposed to be there. It's bright enough to read the sign. And I've been to this place before, screwing around with my friends, but only during the daytime (Redfern-Huberty, interview, 2017).

The light-hearted, fun-fueled evening was soon to change, as Huberty makes vividly clear. Something was about to happen that he was destined never to forget.

As we got closer, maybe about 25 yards away, standing against the sign was a humanoid form that was a shadow; absolutely a shadow. *Dark and tall* [author's italics]. I'm thinking, I'm seeing something, but maybe it's a tree. But, me and the two girls, we had a really dark feeling about it. It really did feel like I was looking at something evil; that's just how it felt. All of a sudden, and as we get closer, I'm going from joking around with the girls, and talking about this stuff, and kind of wanting to get the girls scared, when suddenly...*there it is*. I'm like, it must be my imagination. I could see parts of the sign, but it was like the shadow thing would not reflect light. It was a shadow of something, but as if it was sucking the light in. I look over at the two girls, who are flanking me. And they see it, too. They are frozen in fear, both of them. And, they're just staring at it. Then, they just turn around and run. I ran, too. But, we saw it; the three of us. And, it wasn't like it was just there for just a second. It was *there*-there. Until we looked away and it was gone (Ibid.).

That the tall and shadowy thing encountered by Mike Huberty and his friends in 1993 was seen only eight miles from the location of the almost fatal May 31, 2014 attack on Payton Leutner, is, to say the very least, bizarre. At the other end of the scale, it's downright chilling and even synchronistic. And, let's not forget that the shadow-thing seen by Huberty was lurking amid a bunch of trees, which is, of course, one of the most preferred hangouts of the Slenderman, as we've read.

THE TRAGIC TALE OF "LITTLE LORD FAUNTLEROY"

It's now time to take a look at another sinister affair that Mike Huberty has personally investigated, which occurred

Mike Huberty: "The shadow thing would not reflect light." *Matt Apps, 2017.*

almost a century ago in none other than Waukesha. To this very day, it remains a still-unresolved affair that revolves around the violent death of a young boy. Huberty says, "There are a few horrific stories that center around children, and around Waukesha, too." Indeed, there are (Ibid.).

One such story, says Huberty, was a definitive urban legend. It's one of the kinds that can be found all around the world, regardless of country or culture. It is, however, a potentially important story, as it may well have added to the overall lore surrounding, and the belief in, the air of supernatural menace which has for so long dominated Waukesha and its people. On the matter of this particular story, Huberty states:

> It was the early 1980s, and you had a guy in Illinois who supposedly killed a child, which, of course, made it way more scary. He drove up to this specific place we would go often—the Vernon Marsh, where we saw the shadow thing in 1993— and he dropped the head and the hands and the body off there (Ibid.).

At least, that's how the story goes. Whether based on facts or not, it certainly had people talking. We could make a case based upon the data already discussed in previous chapters that widespread belief in an urban legend might have led to the creation of a Tulpa version of a killer who never really existed. Other accounts investigated by Huberty, however, are far more substantial in nature. One of them, also from Waukesha, revolves around the still-unsolved death of a young, unidentified boy who became known locally as "Little Lord Fauntleroy," and who was named after the lead character in Frances Hodgson Burnett's 1886 novel of the same name. As Huberty notes: "The boy was found with blunt force trauma to the head, but the body was found floating in a quarry." And that was only the start of things (Ibid.).

The story is as mysterious as it is eerie. It also has a Slenderman connection attached to it.

It was on March 8, 1921, that the body of a young boy, violently killed by a powerful and savage blow to the head, was found in Waukesha, specifically in the murky and dirty waters of an old quarry that was, by then, extensively flooded. The quarry was located next to what was called the O'Laughlin Stone Company. Very little could be initially determined, primarily because the body of the child was in a very poor state of decay and bloated, which indicated that it had been in the water for around 10 to 12 weeks; maybe slightly longer, even. What *could* be ascertained for sure, however, was that the boy, estimated to have been around six years of age at the time he was killed, had light-colored hair and wore clothes and shoes that strongly suggested he came from a rich family. Hence the "Little Lord Fauntleroy" title with which the boy became associated.

Despite attempts to ascertain the identity of the child, the mystery of who he was, and who he was bludgeoned to death by, remained unsolved. Even when the police placed his body on display in Waukesha's funeral home, no one came forward to claim the child's body. Not even a promise of a $1,000 reward did any good, which was certainly a substantial amount of money back then. A local woman, Minnie Conrad, who was emotionally affected by the terrible event to a large degree, stepped in and helped raise money around town to give the poor child a respectable funeral. On occasion, and after the funeral, it was rumored among the people of Waukesha that an unknown woman wearing a red veil would leave a bouquet of flowers on the grave. The remains of the child can be found buried in Waukesha's Prairie Home Cemetery, which is barely one-and-a-half miles from David's Park, the site of the Geyser-Weier attack of 2014. There was, however, one curious thing that surfaced at the time—or, to be absolutely specific, that happened shortly *before* the boy was murdered.

In the immediate wake of the discovery of the child's body, one of the O'Laughlin Stone Company's workers approached the Waukesha police and revealed that about a month prior a man and woman had arrived at the facility asking questions; they wanted to know if a young boy had been seen wandering around the local vicinity. Had anyone seen him? Was he taken by anyone? Unfortunately, no one knew anything. While the woman was in a fraught, tearful state, the man walked directly to the quarry and spent a few minutes walking silently around it, intently staring into its waters. The pair vanished as mysteriously as they had first appeared and were never seen again.

It has been suggested that the young boy in question may have been Homer LeMay. He was a little lad who vanished in 1921—the very same year in which the still-unidentified body of the unknown child was found in the old quarry at Waukesha. Homer came from Milwaukee, which is less than 20 miles from Waukesha. Though it must be said that his family was hardly what one could call affluent: Homer's father, Edmond LeMay, worked at the Milwaukee plant of the American Hair and Felt Company. His income wasn't great, so this obviously raises issues about the expensive clothing and shoes the boy was wearing at the time he was killed. Edmond LeMay has been suggested as the murderer on more than a few occasions, too.

According to LeMay, Homer died in Argentina in a car accident while being looked after by a family known as the Nortons. No evidence of any such accident was ever confirmed by Argentinian authorities, though, and the Norton family was never identified. On the other hand, however, there was no solid data to suggest that LeMay had definitely killed his son. He walked free, even though there were major suspicions that he had killed his son. The issue of the man and woman who turned up at the O'Laughlin Stone Company was resurrected. A theory suggested they were Edmond LeMay and his wife. There is sense in that theory since the woman was in a state of complete distress, which is natural, given that it may have been Mrs. LeMay. The man headed straight off to the water-filled quarry, where what may have been Homer's body was found. Perhaps if it was Edmond Lemay who silently stood over the quarry, he was checking to see if the body of his son could be seen. And on the matter of Edmond LeMay's wife, there is this: It's a fact that two of LeMay's three wives died; one allegedly as a result of tuberculosis. The other, Celia, mysteriously vanished amid rumors that LeMay had murdered her.

It's intriguing to note that in 2015 a psychic named Marie St. Claire sought to solve the riddle of Little Lord Fauntleroy once and for all by using definitively psychic means. She identified and described the killer of the young boy as "a slim man in a dark suit." Does that remind you of anyone? Notably, St. Claire also described psychically seeing the body of the child carried by the "slim man" through a stretch of woods—one of the preferred domains of the Slenderman. The location of the killing was only a stone's throw from David's Park, where, in May 2014, yet *another* slim man dressed in a dark-colored suit became an integral player in the stabbing of Payton Leutner. Or, was it the very same character in black haunting Waukesha for decades? (Saint Claire, 2015).

FROM THE WATER MAN TO THE SMILEY-FACED MAN

Mike Huberty has also made an extensive study of a supernatural entity in the area of Waukesha known as the Water Man. Huberty says:

> The legend was brought over to the States by Slavic immigrants in the Midwest [who first came to the United States in the 18th century]. It was of something called the Water Man. He lives in a hidden lair in the deepest part of the rivers. He walks and talks like a normal man and has a cloak that is

split in the back. But the handkerchief that hangs out of his pocket is always dripping wet. I connected this to Slenderman because of his tentacles, his tendrils. The Water Man has hairs on its head—like tentacles—that will drag you into the water. So, the symbolism, the visual, of the tendrils was definitely something kind of similar to Slenderman (Redfern-Huberty, interview, 2017).

In the original Slavic tales, the Water Man, known within Slavic legend as the *Vodyanoy*, is an extremely dangerous creature; it's one to be avoided at all costs possible. He is driven to entice people to the water's edge, at which point those terrible tendrils lunge forward and pull his hysterical, terrified victims into the depths of the river, pond, lake, or stream in which the Vodyanoy lurks and slaughters. Although essentially humanoid in form, the Water Man is clearly not what anyone could call human; his face is like that of a toad or a frog. His paw-like hands are webbed, and he has gills, rather than lungs. In fact, he sounds not unlike the kind of thing that H.P. Lovecraft (one of Eric Knudsen's go-to guys for the Slenderman imagery) might have written about after a particularly fraught night of terrible dreams.

Now, we get to the heart of the story: In pursuing the legends of the Vodyanoy, Mike Huberty stumbled upon a strange series of drownings in the Fox River, which flows past none other than Waukesha. They are drownings that have been attributed to the Water Man and also to a character known as the Smiley-Faced Man—neither of which it would be wise to cross paths with.

A CATALOG OF SMILING MONSTERS

On the matter of the curious deaths by drowning, Huberty shares the following:

> There's an area near Waukesha, the Fox River; a river that runs through the city. The Fox River ran right through the sub-division that Allison and I grew up in. When I was doing research on the drownings, I found we had a bunch of unsolved deaths. They were called the "smiley-faced murders." First, it was all these young men—20, 25 years old—along the Mississippi River; they were mysteriously drowning. There were searches for them, and sometimes it was months before they were found. So, I wondered if there was anything like this on the Fox River. I found 17 documented drownings in the Fox River. I made the connection between the drownings and the folklore of the Water Man (Ibid.).

The story that Huberty dug into is indeed a very strange one. It revolves around the controversial deaths of dozens of men in the American mid-west—the overwhelming majority of whom, at the time, were in their late teens and their early-to-mid-20s. They were deaths that spanned, in total, almost a dozen states. Given the fact that many of the deaths occurred on weekend nights, and more than a few of the victims had alcohol in their systems, a substantial number of the deaths were simply relegated to unfortunate circumstances; namely, guys wobbly walking home late at night, after knocking back a few shots on the weekend, and almost endlessly falling into rivers—and always unable to save themselves from watery deaths. Of course, such a theory is not at all impossible, but a pair of New York police detectives who, after retirement, chose to examine the cases at much closer quarters came to believe that something else was afoot; something much more sinister.

Those detectives were Anthony Duarte and Kevin Gannon. They came to believe that the killer was what has variously been termed as the Smiley Man, the Smiley Face Gang, and the Smiley Face Killer(s)—titles that suggest there may have been more than one killer. As for the "Smiley" connection to all of this, it stemmed from the fact that on more than a few occasions, and near to where the bodies were found, someone had spray-painted on various buildings and walls the famous smiley face that is known to just about one and all. This was seen by Gannon and Duarte as a likely sign that they were dealing with a serial killer. Certainly, serial killers are known to have a near-obsessive drive to leave a few clues as to who they are.

Getting back to Mike Huberty, it's worth noting that eight of the deaths were investigated by the La Crosse,

Wisconsin, Police Department. La Crosse is less than 200 miles from Waukesha. And let's not forget that there were 17 drownings in the Fox River, which runs through Waukesha itself. Nevertheless, the La Crosse police did not buy into the conclusions of Gannon and Duarte. They blamed it all on the booze.

The smiley-face angle to all of this is notable, as there are more than a few paranormal entities that sport what can only be termed terrifying, maniacal grins. One is Indrid Cold, a sinister Man in Black–type character with an undeniably Dickensian-like name. He roamed around the city of Point Pleasant, West Virginia, in the late 1960s when the Mothman affair was at its height. Those who encountered this unsettling entity—usually at night—were unable to take their eyes off of his psychotic, serial-killer-like smile. Today, we have a modern-day equivalent of Indrid Cold. He is, most appropriately, known as the Grinning Man. Imagine Jack Nicholson's insane, grinning character of Jack Torrance in Stanley Kubrick's 1980 movie, *The Shining*, and toss in a liberal amount of MIB, and you'll get the picture. And, then, there are creepy killer clowns. Guaranteed to provoke nightmares just about everywhere, they are, as their title suggests, characters in full-on clown costume and make-up, but who have nothing but your death in mind. And they will be smiling when they snuff out your life. You can bet on that.

WAUKESHA'S CURSED FARM

Now it's time to take a trip back in time to the latter part of the 19th century. Notably, the location of all the carnage to which you are about to be exposed in all of its horrific glory was just a few miles southwest of Waukesha, and alongside the Fox River—both associated with supernatural activity. It all revolves around the Hille Farm, a 250-acre piece of land owned by John Hille, a farmer for whom life was good, until, that is, a series of almost unbelievable and diabolical events occurred that would not be forgotten. Like so many tales coming out of Waukesha and in the vicinity of the winding, old Fox River, this tale, too, is a veritable smorgasbord of death, supernatural activity, and tragedy. It's also one of Mike Huberty's favorite cases.

All was good for the family until the year 1898 when John Hille's wife, Magdalena, was struck down with a mysterious illness that no one could diagnose. Very oddly, Magdalena's doctor mistakenly killed her when he administered not medicine but a lethal poison. The family was utterly devastated, and John Hille soon died as well after falling into a deep depression and refusing to eat. He was soon taken by the Grim Reaper; that he was aged in the extreme at the time probably didn't help. This left the family's six children to ensure that the farm continued to prosper. It has to be said that they failed miserably; although, in fairness, and as will now become apparent, the odds were massively stacked against them from the very beginning.

And when those same odds are clearly saturated by supernatural phenomena, the chances of a positive outcome are slim.

One of the sons, who had a number of physical handicaps, passed away. Another, Oscar, was killed on the property by a large bull. He was crushed to an absolute pulp by the marauding, crazed beast; his internal organs were pummeled beyond saving. Two of the still-then-surviving children of John and Magdalena—Hulda and William—also met grisly ends. The family was originally from Germany and a local man, Elder Krause, who was in their employ, threatened to tell the authorities that they were German spies. This all took place during World War I, so that threat effectively meant that Hulda and William could have found themselves in deep trouble. The truth, though, was that the family was utterly loyal to the United States and Krause was simply engaged in a callous piece of blackmail, along with a neighboring boy, Ernest Fentz.

On one particular day, Krause turned up the heat and demanded money, and lots of it. William well and truly flipped his lid: He took his shotgun and blew away half of Fentz's face. Krause fled the scene. But, William was far from done. He marched to the barn and killed his pet dog and five horses, after which he then killed himself with the very same shotgun. Hulda followed suit and took her life by swallowing a large mouthful of poison and savagely slashing her wrists, thus ensuring her a painful death.

For the next two decades, the Hille Farm remained empty, which is not exactly surprising when one considers the notoriety and unbridled death that was attached to the old farm. But in 1932, a man by the name of Pratt blew himself to smithereens while dynamiting rocks on the property. He surely should have known better than to blast rocks at the site of so many deaths. Pratt clearly didn't think of the possibility of becoming the farm's next victim. Sixteen years later, Ralph and Dorothy Ransome bought the farm. They too should have known better. Five years later, their daughter, Anita, and their son-in-law Andrew Kennedy, moved into Hille Farm. Both of their children were destined to die young: In 1963, seven-year-old Philip drowned in Lake Mondota in Madison, Wisconsin. Then, in 1972, five-year-old Ransome Kennedy was crushed to death by a piece of farm machinery in the very same barn where William Hille killed himself and his beloved animals.

Mike Huberty notes something significant: "The last person to own the farm [in 1972] talked about seeing a shadowy figure wandering around the property." Wonder who that could have been?

Huberty rounds things up with these words: "To know that we have cursed farms, the Smiley murders, shadowy figures, Little Lord Fauntleroy, Slenderman, and child violence and deaths *all* in this area, it makes me ask: Is there some kind of curse in Waukesha?"

A curse of the Slenderman? Given what we know about him, the question is one which should not be dismissed lightly.

14

"I KNEW IT WOULD BE NECESSARY TO KILL HER"

wo young girls. A mysterious and tall figure in black. Murder and mayhem solidly in mind. A savage attack in a picturesque park. And a fantasy world come to life. You may be wondering: Why are we once again focusing on the shocking May 31, 2014 attack on Payton Leutner by Anissa Weier and Morgan Geyser? Well, the answer to that question is: *We're not*. Amazingly, there was an incredibly similar attack way back in 1954 and on the other side of the world in New Zealand. In fact, so eerily similar are the two affairs, it's almost impossible not to ponder on the theory that an early incarnation of the Slenderman was around long before the fascination for today's monster was swirling around in the minds of anyone.

It's a strange story that began in 1952 with a man named Harold H. Fulton, who died in 1986. Back in 1952, Fulton was a sergeant in the Royal New Zealand Air Force and established the New Zealand-based Civilian Saucer Investigation. It was an organization dedicated to investigating the UFO phenomenon. The CSI proved to be an extremely successful venture for Fulton: In less than a year, he had more than 500 subscribers to his journal, which went by the title of *Flying Saucers*.

It wasn't long after the revelations concerning Albert Bender's torturous encounters with the Men in Black surfaced (see Chapter 5) that Fulton contacted Bender. A lengthy period of correspondence between the two duly followed. Indeed, Fulton had established a connection with numerous UFO researchers in the United States, including Gray Barker, who, in 1962, published Albert Bender's MIB-themed book, *Flying Saucers and the Three Men*.

THE FULTON FAMILY GETS TARGETED BY THE SUPERNATURAL

The letters between Fulton and Bender (in my possession) make one thing very clear: Fulton was concerned that whatever it was that had got its grips into Bender was, by the summer of 1953, now doing exactly the same with him. Fulton told Bender (and MIB investigator/author

Gray Barker, too) that on several occasions he experienced in his home the very same overpowering odor of sulfur-meets-rotten-eggs that Bender had talked about. Equally disturbing, Fulton began to see vague, shadowy, human-like figures out of his peripheral vision, usually late at night, and always when he was engaged in his UFO research. They were wizened, goblin-like things that creeped around Fulton's home in what amounted to almost a taunting fashion: They wanted to be seen, but not too closely. A bad sign that the Shadow People were on the move, perhaps?

Then, in August 1953, Fulton and his wife both experienced that overpowering odor together as it filled their entire house. Only a couple of nights later, the pair were woken by the sounds of something pounding hard and violently on one of the walls of their home. And just a couple of nights after that, Mrs. Fulton saw an orange-pink ball of light hovering near the door to their bedroom. It was a period of highly disturbing proportions and unsettling manifestations all rolled into one. Fulton, however, was not the only New Zealand-based UFO investigator to find himself up to his neck in supernatural weirdness. There were others too. And their encounters were no less worrying.

A STRANGE VOICE AND DEMONIC ACTIVITY

Late one night in 1952, Fulton confided in Albert Bender that a researcher from Hamilton, New Zealand, named John Stuart—author of *UFO Warning*—had a somewhat unsettling, recent experience that had severely messed with his nerves. Midnight was closing in when Stuart, fast asleep in bed at the time, was jolted awake by the sound of the phone ringing. Of course, and quite naturally, the first thing to cross Stuart's mind was that it was someone calling him with bad news. Well, in a very strange way, it *was*, but not the kind of bad news that you might expect to receive in the early hours. The eerie and almost-robotic voice at the other end of the line warned Stuart to quit digging into the UFO mystery or be prepared to pay a very heavy price. The phone then went dead. Gray Barker later wrote that after the call, Stuart poured himself a stiff drink to calm his nerves. No doubt! Robert S. Ellwood, the author of *Islands of the Dawn: The Story of Alternative Spirituality in New Zealand*, said of the mysterious voice that it was as if "some kind of machine had learned to talk." That, however, was not the only encounter of the sinister kind that Stuart found himself in (Ellwood, 1993).

In 1953, Stuart worked closely with a woman named Doreen Wilkinson, who shared Stuart's passion for UFOs. There may have been other passions at work, too. Certainly, there were hushed rumors among New Zealand's closely knit UFO research community that Stuart, a married man, and Doreen were far more than just good friends. They were rumors that they both vehemently denied. Maybe, they denied those same rumors just a tad too vehemently. We'll never know.

What went unknown for a long time was that on a number of occasions in the early hours of the morning, which was typically when the pair did their research, Doreen seemed to take on a different personality. It was one of a sexual seductress. Stuart was, at first, of the opinion that this was due to the manipulative powers of aliens, who he believed may have been interested in the nature of human sexuality, and who were somehow actively controlling Doreen's mind and body. Stuart soon came to think something very different, however: Doreen was periodically under the possession of a literal demonic entity that was masquerading as an extraterrestrial—according to Harold Fulton, at least, who had picked up on various portions of the story and then passed them on to Albert Bender.

Things only got progressively worse. Late one night a wild and diabolical, hair-covered humanoid creature manifested right inside Stuart's home. The "conspicuously male entity," as the tale tactfully worded it, made a move on terrified Doreen, but then inexplicably vanished. Then, a couple of nights later, when she was alone, Doreen was reportedly violently raped by an invisible creature as she lay naked on her bed. There was, however, evidence that this was not just the product of the human mind: Doreen was covered in small, unexplained scratches. Perhaps not surprisingly, both John and Doreen walked away from Ufology. Maybe, even, they ran. After all, who could blame them for that? (Ellwood, 1993)

With this brief but tumultuous history of the very early years of New Zealand Ufology, it's time to return to the research of Harold Fulton and a certain slender figure in dark clothes.

A TALL STRANGER IN BLACK

It's important to note that Albert Bender and Gray Barker were not the only people with personal interests in the Men in Black and who Harold Fulton contacted and corresponded with. Fulton was very familiar with the writings of Harold T. Wilkins, and owned a copy of Wilkins's 1954 book, *Flying Saucers on the Attack*. Fulton, after having read Wilkins's book, wrote to Wilkins (care of his publisher, Ace Star Books) and related an extraordinary story to Wilkins that, with the benefit of hindsight, has a major bearing upon the Slenderman enigma. Given the fact that Fulton was hardly a stranger to the Men in Black phenomenon, it's not surprising at all that he chose to confide in Wilkins.

Although Gray Barker's 1956 book *They Knew Too Much About Flying Saucers* was the first, full-length book on the MIB mystery, the fact that (as noted in Chapter 5) Wilkins's book contained an early, archetypal, tentacled Man in Black case with Slenderman overtones attached to it prompted Fulton to correspond with Wilkins. It was for this reason that Fulton chose to share the story with Wilkins, rather than with Barker, whose own book was still very much in the process of being researched and which would not be published for another two years.

According to what Fulton had to say to Wilkins, on a number of occasions between the latter part of April and mid-May 1954, a mysterious character was seen walking around the city's green and pleasant Victoria Park, which is situated in the expansive Port Hills, and that overlooked the city of Christchurch. The man in question (if he was indeed a man and not something much more dangerous) was described by those who saw him as being dressed in a black suit and tie. He wore a black fedora *and was very thin and tall*: somewhere in the region of six-and-half-feet in height. Rather significantly, but also very disturbingly, the man's modus operandi was to approach children playing in the park and then engage them in conversation.

Ominously, Fulton continued to Wilkins that the man was said to have some sort of hypnotic sway over those kids that he targeted. It's not surprising, then, that parents would quickly usher their transfixed children away.

Perhaps the tall man in the black suit was just a lonely soul, looking for someone to talk to, but unwittingly provoking fear in the process. Or, maybe, he wasn't. There's a possibility, of course, that he was a dangerous, sexual predator; someone to be avoided at all costs. But what convinced Fulton that there might have been a different explanation is the fact that, according to one woman who Fulton had the opportunity to interview firsthand, the

BRIDGEPORT 4, CONN.
U. S. A.
May 5, 1954

Mr. Harold H. Fulton
Pres. C.S.I. of N.Z.
P. O. Box 1914,
Auckland, New Zealand

Dear Harold:

Sorry that I have not written to you long before this, but I
have been quite busy with many things involving the publication,
visits to Washington, D.C. in regards to things I know, and also
with preparations for my forthcoming wedding to a charming English
lass from merry old England.

So happy to know that you do not believe all the idle stories that
are circulating in regards to IFSB. It seems a shame that some
are not satisfied·with pushing me into the dirt, but they must also
drag me through it. I have noted many instances where remarks
have been made that are certainly uncalled for. However, what can
you do under the circumstances. Everyone is subjected to ridicule
in these trying times.

I might add that when the time comes for the secret to be known
the whole world will be amazed and astounded by what they shall
learn.

Rest assured Harold that when I am able to tell anything you will
be one of the first to know it, because you have been always fair
and understanding.

I have always admired your group for its fine work and hope that
just because I am no longer in saucer work, that we can remain
on as good friends as we have in the past.

Under separate cover I am mailing you copies of our last release.

Please write to me again when you have time, and I would like to
send you an article for your publication if you will accept same.

Very truly yours,

Your friend,

Al Bender

Letter from Albert Bender to Harold Fulton, 1954. *Albert Bender,
May 5, 1954.*

giant in black vanished before her terror-filled eyes. As in *dematerialized*. There was, then, clearly something sinister and supernatural afoot in the tree-shrouded confines of Victoria Park. And it all revolved around a dark-suited, skinny Goliath who was drawn to children.

The events in question were overshadowed when, just a few weeks later, a shocking murder was committed in the very same park: *by two young girls who lived in a fantasy world*. Their names were Juliet Hulme and Pauline Parker, the former was just 15 years old at the time and the latter 16 years old. And they achieved unsurprising worldwide notoriety after they savagely killed Parker's mother, Honora. But how did the two girls come to commit so savage an attack? And why? That's a long and winding story all of its own. The story is so close to that of Morgan Geyser, Anissa Weier, and Payton Leutner that it's practically jaw-dropping.

FROM FRIENDSHIP TO TRAGEDY

Juliet Hulme and Pauline Parker, both of the city of Christchurch, had radically different backgrounds. Juliet's father was Henry Rainsford Hulme, a well-respected physicist and someone who was an integral player in the development of the United Kingdom's hydrogen bomb. Originally from the U.K., Hulme and his family moved to New Zealand in 1948, when Juliet was just nine. Upon arriving in a new land, Henry Hulme immediately took on the prestigious position of the rector of Christchurch's University of Canterbury, which was founded back in 1873. In contrast, Parker came from a solidly working-class background: Her mother and father ran a fish store in the city. There was, however, one thing that ensured the pair had a deep and lasting tie: ill health.

As a young girl, Hulme was struck down by tuberculosis, which can cause serious and sometimes fatal damage to the lungs. Parker had osteomyelitis, a condition that provokes inflammation and infection in the bones. In a strange fashion, it was their afflictions that helped to bring the girls together. As for where they met, it was at the Christchurch Girls High School. Both families were pleased that the girls became good friends so quickly. They spent more and more time together and, eventually, were completely inseparable. It was this latter point which eventually led to rumors that, by the time of the murder, their relationship had gone from one of deep friends to a physical, sexual one.

As their connection deepened, the girls turned their backs on mainstream religion, which they were taught in their school, and chose to create their very own fantasy realm. It was a land they called *The Fourth World*. It was, one might say, another dimension; a strange environment into which the girls believed they could enter when they were in particular altered states of mind. *The Fourth World* was a place that had its own form of faith, rules, and history. Fictional characters were intricately created and woven into *The Fourth World* mythology, and who became part of everyday life for the girls. They wrote at length in their journals about the mysterious world just beyond ours. The lines between reality and imagination were becoming intricately intertwined. It was then that things started to spiral into chaos, stress, and—ultimately—a life extinguished.

A DIARY OF DEATH

Concerned that the girls were perhaps becoming just a bit *too* close (we are talking about an unenlightened era when same-sex relationships were deeply frowned upon) all four parents decided to try and restrict the girls' time spent together. Bad move. *Very* bad. Resentment and hatred started to set in for both of the girls. Things got even worse for them when, in the early part of 1954, Dr. Hulme and his wife decided to divorce and, as a result, the doctor made plans to return to the United Kingdom. As for Juliet, she was destined for somewhere very different: South Africa. The family had relatives there and it was felt that the hot climate would be good for Juliet's tuberculosis and her general health.

Pauline, panicky and realizing that she was about to be separated from her best friend, pleaded to go to South Africa with Juliet. It all proved to be of no avail. So, the girls took drastic action to try and prevent them being separated. It was a drastic action of just about the worst kind possible. And it spelled the end of their friendship.

The build-up to what turned out to be a terrible death for Pauline Parker's mother, Honora, was disturbing. That much is evidenced from certain entries contained in Pauline's journal, which became part of the evidence presented by the prosecution team after the two were arrested. On February 13, 1954, Pauline wrote that her mother was becoming a major problem for her. As court records notes, she asked herself, in chilling words, "Why could not mother die? Dozens of people are dying, thousands are dying every day. So why not mother and father too?" (Furneaux, 1955).

By April, Pauline was referring to her mother as nothing less than an obstacle, and was determined to get rid of her. Then, just three days before the killing took place, Pauline wrote in her journal that she and Juliet had "worked it all out and are both thrilled with the idea. Naturally we feel a trifle nervous but the anticipation is great." Those chilling words would soon be read to a hushed courtroom of people (Ibid.).

Overwhelming derangement was clearly setting in and taking a firm and crushing grip on the two friends.

MURDER IN THE PARK

On the morning of the 22nd—the day on which Honora Parker was to destined to be killed—Pauline penned the following, which was also entered into the official court records: "I felt very excited and the night-before-Christmassy last night. I did not have pleasant dreams, though. I am about to rise" (Ibid.).

The girls had things planned down to an absolute tee: They pretended they had finally come to terms with being separated and, as a result, asked Pauline's mother if they could say their fond farewells to each other on the inviting slopes of the Port Hills, specifically in Victoria Park—the recent abode of a certain, tall creep in black who pursued children. To Honora's eternal cost, she agreed. After a pleasant lunch, the three women—Pauline, Juliet, and Honora—strolled to a nearby bus stop and took a ride to Cashmere, which was followed by a mile-long walk to the park. All seemed perfectly normal; the three even had afternoon tea together. But, the Grim Reaper, knowing what was afoot, was waiting eagerly in the shadows. It would only be a few more minutes before he would have yet another soul to take. The tension was rising…and rising.

After tea, the trio took a short walk across a small hill, along a dirt path, and then into the heart of a plantation on the hills. It was then, amid a brief argument between mother and daughter, that all of the fury, hatred, and resentment that the pair had for Honora exploded in bloody, pulverizing fashion.

The pair took a house brick, wrapped it in a stocking, pushed Honora on to the ground, and then repeatedly smashed the brick into Honora's head. Forensics showed that she had been forcibly held down by her throat when the attack began. Honora's head was so badly damaged that parts of her skull could be seen. Her jaw was violently knocked out of place and shattered. One of Honora's fingers was all but severed, which was perceived by the police's forensics team as evidence that she had fought to save her life by trying to deflect the fury-driven blows. All in all, there were more than 40 injuries to Honora's head and body. It was a terrible way to die.

The girls left Honora's body where it lay and then ran to the park's kiosk. The court records refer to Pauline as having screamed to the kiosk staff: "Please help. Mother has fallen and hit her head on a rock and is covered in blood. I think she is dead." The body was found by a man named Kenneth Ritchie, who was married to the managers of the kiosk. It was a horrific sight, to be sure ("Parker-Hulme Murder Case," 2017).

The Christchurch police were quickly on the scene. Pauline tried to convince the officers that her mother "twisted sideways and hit her head on a rock or something. She seemed to keep tossing up and down and hitting her head." It didn't take the astute police long at all to realize that this was no accident. The tale the girls told was beyond unlikely. Indeed, the police were having none of it. The girls soon had murder charges hanging over their heads. Juliet soon admitted: "After the first blow was struck I knew it would be necessary to kill her. I was terrified and hysterical" (Ibid.).

Their combined fates were now very close to being sealed. It was all just a matter of time. And time, for the girls, was now rapidly running out.

GUILT, SEPARATION, INCARCERATION, AND NEW LIVES

One week before the end of August 1954, the trial was underway. For five days, testimony, deliberation, and a comprehensive study of all of the available information were the collective name of the game. The defense used insanity as the explanation for the killing. A Dr. Reginald Medlicott was brought in by the defense team. He told the court: "The crown has seen fit to refer to the accused as ordinary dirty-minded little girls. Our evidence will show that they are nothing of the kind. The Crown's description is unfortunate and medically incorrect. They are mentally sick girls more to be pitied than to be blamed" (Drayton, 2016).

Dr. Medlicott went on to suggest that the pair were suffering from "paranoia of the exalted type…a form of systemized delusional insanity." He also noted that "As the diary goes on evil becomes more and more important and one gets the feeling that they ultimately become helpless under its sway." By the time of the attack, the doctor added, in his opinion both girls were "grossly insane" (Medlicott, 1955).

The prosecution brought in psychiatrists who presented the jury with a very different scenario: The girls were 100 percent sane, were cold and calculating, and knew *exactly* what they were doing when they took Honora's life. The jury was far more convinced by the prosecution's argument than they were by that of the defense team. On the fifth day, the jury had made up their minds: Both girls were found guilty of murder. Because of their young ages, however, they were jailed for five years each, rather than being hung by the neck, as was the customary sentence for murder in New Zealand at the time. They were immediately separated and never, ever saw each other again.

SIMILARITIES OF THE BIZARRE KIND

Regardless of one's own personal opinion on what lies at the heart of the Slenderman enigma, there can be no doubting the deep and incredible parallels between the events in Waukesha, Wisconsin, on May 31, 2014, and those which went down in Victoria Park, Christchurch, New Zealand, on June 22, 1954, which was some 60 years earlier. In both cases, we have two girls with a close bond. Pauline Parker and Juliet Hulme created their own fantasy land known as *The Fourth World*. It was filled with fictional characters that—in the minds of the girls, at least—had far more than a semblance of reality attached to them. Morgan Geyser and Anissa Weier had an obsession with the world's most dangerous and fictional character, the Slenderman. In the same way that *The Fourth World* was filled with fantastic realms, for Geyser and Weier the dark and fantasy-filled depths of the Nicolet National Forest were where the Slenderman's sprawling mansion could be found. And the parallels don't end there.

In both the 1954 affair and that of 2014, the victim was violently attacked by two young girls. Both attacks occurred in parks. New Zealander Doreen Wilkinson, who knew Harold T. Wilkins's informant, Harold Fulton, was supernaturally assaulted in her bedroom by an invisible entity that left scratch marks on her body. Morgan Geyser's mother said that her daughter had told her how ghosts appeared in her bedroom at night, pulling on her hair and biting her body. And, of course, there is the matter of the tall and thin character that was seen in Christchurch's Victoria Park in the weeks leading up to the death of Honora Parker.

It would be foolish in the extreme for us to dismiss all of the above as nothing more than mere coincidence. Supernatural synchronicity of the kind we saw earlier? Certainly.

Today, Juliet Hulme lives in the United States under the name of Anne Perry. She has written dozens of successful mystery/murder-based novels; a subject of which she clearly has personal knowledge and experience. Pauline Parker moved to the U.K. and lives a quiet life.

15

"A TALL, DARK, AND TERRIFYING ENTITY"

The Cannock Chase is a large area of thick woodland, expansive fields, green hills, bubbling streams, and long and winding centuries-old canals in the English county of Staffordshire. Shugbrough Hall, which dates back to 1693, is a huge stately home that sits on the fringes of the Chase and which resembles the kind of old house you might expect to see on the likes of *Downton Abbey*. Even older are the remains of what is known as Castle Ring. It's an Iron Age–era hill-fort that was inhabited by the Cornovii people more than 2,000 years ago. It overlooks much of

Staffordshire from its prominent position on the Chase at a height of almost 800 feet. Large numbers of wild deer roam the Cannock Chase, and the entire area is a mecca for dog-walkers and joggers. In other words, the area is as inviting as it is picturesque. But, don't let yourself be deceived. All is not well on the Cannock Chase, not in the slightest.

For years, sightings have been made on the Chase of ghostly, fiery-eyed black dogs—the malevolent and supernatural kind that inspired Sir Arthur Conan Doyle to pen his classic Sherlock Holmes novel *The Hound of the Baskervilles*, which was published in 1902. Large black cats, the size of mountain lions, no less, have been seen prowling around the Cannock Chase German Military Cemetery. In 2007, the very same cemetery caught the local media's attention when a handful of locals reported seeing a marauding, large creature that can only be described as a werewolf. Bigfoot-type entities and hairy "wild men" have been seen in the area for centuries as well. There are even accounts of strange, large, slithering monsters in some of the large and murky bodies of water on the Chase. Mothman-type things have been encountered too. It truly is a lair of monsters, and certainly not a place to venture into after the sun has set and darkness has enveloped the land. There is another monstrous thing that has been seen lurking on and around the Cannock Chase on more than a few occasions. You know the one, right? Sure, you do.

DISORIENTATION AND TERROR

What is particularly interesting about the Cannock Chase Slenderman reports is that some of them pre-date 2009, which was when Eric Knudsen unleashed the infernal thing on the Internet. A prime example is a fascinating and unsettling story from a local man named Mike Johnson. It was in June 2001 that Johnson's path crossed with that of the Slenderman. At the time in question, Johnson was working on a project with the Staffordshire Wildlife Trust and the University of Wolverhampton, specifically in relation to the area's flora and vegetation. Notably, when Johnson had his encounter with the Slenderman, he was only a stone's throw away from the aforementioned and supernaturally saturated Cannock Chase German Military Cemetery.

It was a warm, bright, early afternoon, with barely a cloud in the sky, and Johnson was seeking out an area that was home to an abundance of what is known as Midland Hawthorn, a large shrub, which can grow to a height of around 25 feet. Everything was normal until Johnson noticed something very strange: There was a sudden and overwhelming silence. The whistling and chirping of the birds in the area came to an ominous halt. Even the sounds of the many cars and trucks that regularly negotiate the Chase's winding roads were completely non-existent. The term "deafening silence" accurately describes the immediate situation that Johnson found himself in.

At first, Johnson didn't think too much of it, relegating the odd, and admittedly somewhat eerie, situation to just one of those things (whatever those "things" might be). In moments, a herd of around 50 or so deer appeared on a ridge in the distance, something that put a smile on Johnson's face as he watched them run. Their destination appeared to be a large plantation of woodland to the right of Johnson. Maybe, they realized something was on their collective tails—something they were determined to flee from. Then, as Johnson continued to watch, something very weird, even terrifying, happened.

Although Johnson knew the Cannock Chase like he knew the back of his own hand, he found himself unable to figure out where he was, despite having been to the area on many occasions. It was, to be sure, an extremely unnerving feeling. A track that he took toward the cemetery should have been to the east of him. It was now to the west. Even the sun was out of place: At that time of the day, around 2 p.m., Johnson recalled, it should have been high in the west. It was not; it was north of his position. Feeling disoriented and with a degree of rising panic, Johnson realized that something was *very* wrong. He quickly grabbed his compass, which, oddly, was as dead as the proverbial doornail. He became confused as he then tried to compare the surrounding landscape with that on a map he had with him. It was as if a more than subtle shift in the environment had occurred. Not lost on Johnson was the startling fact that he was completely lost, and utterly without moorings, only around 2,000 feet or so from where his car was parked at the old cemetery—a place he knew all too well. Then, as the atmosphere became even more oppressive, our old "friend," the Slenderman, suddenly appeared on the scene.

As Johnson tried to figure out what was happening to not just the landscape but to him, he caught sight of three people out for a walk. Very weirdly, Johnson could hear every word they were saying, despite being a significant distance from them. As they got closer, he could see that one was a man, dressed in light-colored clothes and carrying a rucksack. The other two were women, who Johnson estimated were both around retirement age. Then, without any warning, they vanished right before Johnson's terrified eyes. He tried to rationalize things by thinking they must have descended into a gully. That would be plausible, except for the fact that there was no gully in the area. Even more confusing, just a couple of minutes later the three people reappeared around 600 feet to the left of Johnson. Except now there weren't three of them, there were *four* of them.

Johnson stared at the group with his mouth agape as he realized that the new addition to the group didn't look entirely human. The figure was not just tall, but impossibly massive for a human—somewhere in the region of *nine feet*. He was dressed in a dark gray-colored outfit that fitted him, or *it*, tightly. The thing's head was bald and elongated, and his neck was incredibly long. As for the arms of the entity, they reached past his knees. What was particularly odd was the fact that Johnson could not make out the face of the man-thing. It was as if there *was* no face or that it was somehow blurred. Could things get any stranger? Yes, they could. And they did. As the group got closer, the giant man placed his hand upon the shoulder of one of the women, who failed to respond in the slightest—something which led Johnson to think that the three could not see, or feel the presence of, the creature. It was only visible to Johnson.

And then, with no warning, the experience was over. The foreboding sense of disorientation and confusion that had so overwhelmed Johnson was immediately gone. The birds were singing again. The familiar sounds of traffic returned. The man, the two women, and the Slenderman were nowhere in sight. Relieved, but still highly unnerved by the whole situation, Johnson raced back to the car-park, got in his vehicle, and fled the area. At the time that Johnson told his story, which was in 2007, he had not returned to the location of his encounter with the giant figure. That wasn't quite the end of things, however. Johnson revealed that he had a similar experience in 2002.

ANOTHER MYSTERIOUS EXPERIENCE IN THE WOODS

It's hardly surprising that Mike Johnson spent a great deal of time pondering the nature of the strange experience he had on the Cannock Chase back in 2001. After 16 years, there is one thing he is absolutely sure of: For a few brief minutes there was a less-than-subtle alteration to his immediate environment. He suspects strongly that it was a change that was only noticeable to him. Certainly, the group of walkers he saw—who were briefly "accompanied" by the Slenderman—were clearly not aware of the entity in their midst, nor did they act in a hysterical fashion. For them, it was as if the monster was not there, which was the exact opposite of the state that Johnson found himself in.

While trying to rationalize it all, Johnson is not of the opinion that he possesses what might be termed "extra-normal powers" or "insights." Rather, he suspects that he may just have been in the right area at the same time and that there may have been a brief merging of two distinctly different realities, one of which was our reality and the other being the one from which the Slenderman came. The idea of a kind of inter-dimensional experience is one which Johnson suspects may be the correct one.

The story gets even more intriguing, because Johnson had another odd experience one year later in 2002. On this occasion, the location was far removed from the depths of the Cannock Chase. It was, however, a heavily forested area, the kind of place that clearly attracts the Slenderman.

On this second occasion, the location was Loch Garten, located in the northeast portion of Scotland and which is close to the Cairngorm Mountains. The specific location was an untouched area of Scots pine trees and alder. Once again, Johnson suddenly found himself overwhelmed by a feeling that something was wrong, but couldn't put his finger on exactly what it was; there was no giant, skinny figure. Johnson didn't find himself confused and unable to negotiate the landscape. It was just a nagging feeling that the atmosphere of those enchanting woods had somehow shifted. And not in a particularly good way. Since then, something broadly similar happens to Johnson several times a year.

What can we say with certainty about Johnson's experience on the Cannock Chase in 2001? Undoubtedly, something very strange happened to him on that fateful June afternoon. What should have been a regular, even relaxing day at work quickly became something else entirely. The sense of disorientation, and the feeling that reality has somehow shifted, are classic aspects of encounters with the Slenderman. Most significant of all, however, is the fact that Johnson was able to accurately describe the physical appearance of the Slenderman in 2007, which was a full *two years* before Eric Knudsen created it. Consider the story of Johnson: The entity he saw was around nine feet in height. Its arms were incredibly long. The head of the thing was totally hairless. It was dressed in a dark gray outfit. And its face was, well, face*less*. Put all of those aspects together and you have what is undeniably a perfect description of the Slenderman, but which was seen way back in the summer of 2001.

The Slenderman haunts the Cannock Chase woods. *Nick Redfern, 2014.*

There is something else that is well worth noting: Johnson's second encounter occurred in Scotland near the Cairngorm Mountains. It just so happens that particular mountain range has a legend of a malevolent entity attached to it: a tall and dark figure known as the "Big Gray Man."

A SCOTTISH SLENDERMAN?

A huge and imposing range, the Cairngorms are filled with an air of mystery, and particularly so one mountain that goes by the name of Ben Macdui. It is on Ben Macdui, more than any other peak in the range, that most of the encounters with the Big Gray Man have occurred. Although some researchers have suggested that the BGM might be some form of Scottish Bigfoot, a careful and in-depth study of the overall phenomenon shows that, in reality, most witnesses describe seeing a large, human figure, but one that seems far more shadowy-like, even silhouetted in some cases. Like the Slenderman, the Big Gray Man seems to have the ability to control and manipulate the human mind: People talk of sudden and overwhelming panic grabbing them and refusing to let go. Almost always, the tortured witnesses are only able to break the spell by fleeing for their lives down the treacherous mountain, and until the point when they are finally out of the reach of the grip of the Big Gray Man.

The leading authority on the matter of the Big Gray Man is Andy Roberts, an English researcher and author and also a skilled mountain-climber, who has scaled the Cairngorms on a number of occasions. Roberts's files demonstrate that most of the encounters with the Big Gray Man contain certain key elements, which turn up time and time again. The location is usually shrouded by thick fog. There is a sudden crunching in the snow, as if something large and heavy is in the direct midst of the witness, and is getting closer and closer by the second. It's then that overwhelming terror kicks in, as does a sizeable amount of adrenaline, and the witness runs for his or her life.

As for when the phenomenon of the Big Gray Man began, that's hard to say with complete certainty. Many researchers of the BHM mystery point in the direction of the 1791 experience of a poet named James Hogg, who also worked as a shepherd. Hogg's sighting of a tall entity—surrounded by a halo—has become a classic. Andy Roberts says:

> As he watched the halo which had formed around him due to the combination of sunshine and mist he suddenly noticed a huge, looming figure. It was vaguely human in shape and he imagined it to be the devil. Hogg fled in terror, not stopping until he reached fellow shepherds" (Roberts, 2010).

THE ENCOUNTERS INCREASE

Now, let's return to the Cannock Chase and jump forward in time to 2015. That was when a cluster of Slenderman encounters surfaced in and around the vicinity of the Cannock Chase. Several of those cases were provided to a local, full-time journalist, Lee Brickley, who has made a careful and deep study of the Cannock Chase and its many attendant supernatural mysteries. In January 2015, Brickley stated: "Over the last two months, sightings of a tall, dark, and terrifying entity have been flooding in. The fact that so many people witnessed the same thing during such a short period fascinated me" (Brickley, 2015).

Brickley states that of the cases which he was personally able to investigate, most of them occurred while the witness was at home in bed. Yes, we're talking about something we have seen before: the issue of the Slenderman turning up when the victim is at his mercy and when they are deep in the throes of sleep-paralysis. But not all of the cases that reached Brickley occurred in homes. There were also those that took place in those old and mysterious woods.

One such encounter took place on January 2, 2015. The location was a notable one: the Castle Ring, an Iron Age-era fort, the remains of which can still be seen engraved upon the ancient landscape, even after thousands of years. Such is the magical allure of the Castle Ring, where there have been sightings of Bigfoot-type creatures, ghostly apparitions, and other supernatural phenomena, that people often feel compelled to spend time there, and particularly so at night. Such was the case with one of Brickley's most intriguing cases.

It was late at night, the clear sky was filled with stars, and the landscape was dark—illumination in the immediate area being significantly reduced. The witness told Brickley of seeing a strange figure on the fringes of the Ring. Incredibly, the dark, humanoid figure rose off the ground and for a few moments appeared to be suspended in the air. Interestingly, the witness likened the figure to Spring-Heeled Jack, a terrifying and legendary character that plagued the people of London, England, in the 1800s and the Midlands area of England, too, which just happens to be where the Cannock Chase is sited. There are clear overtones between Spring-Heeled Jack and the Slender-man: both are tall and thin, their clothing is black, and their skin is pale. And they provoke nothing but outright fear in those who cross their paths.

Although it was a dark night, the witness said that there was at least a small degree of illumination coming from the lights of Rugeley, a nearby town. To the absolute terror of the witness, the flying thing came closer. The thing could now be seen for what it was: a humanoid figure, dressed in a long, black coat and wearing a homburg-type hat, which was also black. Its eyes blazed red and as it opened its mouth it brandished savage-looking fangs. In a moment, it dropped to the ground and was gone, to the eternal relief of the witness.

PALE-SKINNED WITH ELONGATED ARMS

Then, there was another case that occurred in 2015. It was around 2 a.m. and the witness, who lived in the vicinity of the Cannock Chase, was woken up by a strange scratching sound in the bedroom. On looking around the room she saw a spherical "shadow" hovering near her closet. It slowly morphed into the form of an approximately eight-foot-tall, pale-skinned figure that the witness said was somewhat vampire-like. In a complete state of shock, the witness fell back to the bed, at which point the arms of the monster stretched and stretched to around twice their normal length—which is something we have seen before in Slenderman cases—and closed in on her. Claws ran down her face, at which point she screamed and the figure retreated into the shadows and was gone.

In another and final 2015 case, the time-frame was very similar: around 2:30 a.m., and the location again was near the Cannock Chase. A loud noise in the bedroom woke the witness, who was terrified to see a floating, humanoid figure over the bed, staring malevolently in an eyes-to-eyes situation. Worst of all, the eyes glowed a fiery red and the thing was dressed completely in black. The witness said that the dark figure spoke to them in telepathic fashion—which is how the Slenderman is said to communicate with his victims—although they did not expand upon what, exactly, was said. Things came to a sudden end when the blazing-eyed monster floated toward the ceiling and suddenly vanished. It seems safe to say that probably not much sleep was had by the witness for the rest of the night.

16

"HIS ARMS ARE IMPOSSIBLY LONG"

avid Weatherly is a renowned author and researcher of many issues of the supernatural kind, including that of the Black-Eyed Children, who are just about as malevolence-filled as the Slenderman. But not even the Black-Eyed Children have succeeded in ousting the Slenderman from its number-one position in the supernatural stakes. Over the last few years, Weatherly has been following the Slenderman controversy and, as a direct result, he has been on the receiving end of more than a few accounts of real-world encounters with the Slenderman—

David Weatherly, who has uncovered a number of Slenderman reports. *Nick Redfern, 2016.*

encounters that are as sinister as they are intriguing. Weatherly has been good enough to share with me certain cases that, in the high-strangeness stakes, really stand out. As is the case with Robin Swope, Weatherly too has cases in his files regarding sightings of the Slenderman decades ago.

We'll start with the story of Matt, a witness to the unearthly, black-suited thing as both a child and as an adult, which indicates that age has very little to do with the issue of when one might encounter the creature. It also suggests that when, as an adult, one moves away from the family home, the Slenderman is still able to track you down and find you. (And endlessly torment you, too.) Bear that in mind if you ever encounter the Slenderman: It may well be equipped with a supernatural equivalent of a sophisticated tracking-device, something along the lines of a GPS.

As Matt told David Weatherly in 2004, it was when Matt was a child—which was long before Eric Knudsen's Slenderman ever became a definitive phenomenon—that he first encountered the Slenderman, and while he was growing up in the state of Ohio. Matt related to Weatherly:

> I remember seeing a figure like this when I was a child in Ohio. I know that I saw it. I remember having horrible dreams for the longest time but my parents kept telling me I was just having nightmares and there really wasn't anything out there. But he was; I know that he was out there every night for a whole summer. He was always standing in the trees at the back of the yard, and from my bed I could see him. I don't know what finally made him go away, but I know that I prayed every night that he wouldn't harm me when I fell asleep (Weatherly, 2016).

Those of a skeptical nature might say that Matt's experiences as a child amount to nothing more than the kinds of nightmares that all young kids get at one time or another; perhaps not unlike horrific dreams of monsters in a shadow-filled closet or of hideous creatures lurking under the bed, ready to surface and pounce on a terrified child. There is, however, a very important thing to note: Matt saw the Slenderman as an adult, too. At the time when the latter encounters took place, Matt was in the final year of his 20s and was living and working in Indiana for a computer company. All was good; the work was not overly taxing and he made a good income. Or, rather, all was good *for a while*. Things have a way of changing, and not always in a particularly good way.

On one specific night, there was a party for one of Matt's friends at work. Matt stressed to David Weatherly that he wasn't drinking at the party, so that wasn't a factor in what happened later that same night. It had been a long day and night, so when Matt got home he planned on going straight to bed; he didn't even turn on the bedroom light. But just as he happened to look out of the window of his bedroom, Matt saw something that immediately took the almost-30-year-old man back to the tumultuous terrors of his childhood days. He was placed into a state of fear as those memories of years long gone flooded and overwhelmed his mind. Right outside, in the yard and amid the darkness of the night, and standing among a couple of trees, was the Slenderman "waving its long arms about." Echoing that childhood mindset and those frightening memories, Matt, instantly terrified, jumped into bed and prayed the creature in black to "just leave me alone" (Ibid.).

Of course, given that the term *Slenderman* was not created until 2009, when Matt gave David Weatherly the details of his encounter, he never mentioned the entity by its now-infamous moniker. Weatherly says that Matt "was never sure what to call it, simply that it was a disturbing being and he wanted no part of it" (Ibid.).

"I HAD THE MOST AWFUL FEELING"

Janet grew up in rural Virginia and is someone who has been absolutely plagued by the Slenderman; there really is no other way to word it. Interestingly, just like Matt and so many others who have encountered the Slenderman, the home in which Janet grew up was dominated by trees. Indeed, behind the house was a large area of thick woodland. But you had probably already guessed that, right? It was when she was around 10 years of age that Janet's life of childhood fun was drastically and adversely impacted by the sudden presence of a tall, thin thing that provoked nothing but fear in her. For reasons that, at first, Janet didn't really understand, she started to wake up in the dead of night, usually around 2 a.m., and on a regular basis. It was a tiring time, being awoken amid a sense of fear, but not really knowing why. It wasn't at all long, though, before Janet found out. The news, as per usual when it comes to the Slenderman, was bad.

On one occasion when, yet again, Janet found herself unable to sleep in the early hours, she heard the distinct sounds of something moving around outside. Fortunately (or maybe not), it was the height of summer and Janet's window was wide open, significantly amplifying the sound. As the bedroom was on the second floor, Janet peered out the window and looked intently into the blackness of the yard. It wasn't so much what Janet *saw*—at least, not at first—but what she *heard* that caught her attention. It was a curious scratching noise. Her first, and quite natural, thought was that it was one of the family's cats scratching against the door, wanting inside. It was then, however, that Janet got the shock of her life. As her eyes became more and more accustomed to the darkness, she could see "something very tall by the trees," specifically where the thick woods began (Ibid.).

"I had the most awful feeling that whatever it was, it was staring at me," Janet told David Weatherly. "I felt really, really afraid and I ran to my bed, ducking under the covers and staying there until morning." Come morning, and the welcoming daylight, Janet convinced herself that the strange event was just a very vivid dream. The events of a couple of years later, though, strongly suggested otherwise (Ibid.).

Janet was fast approaching her teenage years and the family was still in the same house, so she still had the same bedroom; yes, the very same one that gave a good view of those ominous, haunting woods. After a period of several years of uninterrupted sleep, Janet started to experiences disturbances to her sleep yet again. This time, she was waking up at just about any time between approximately 1 a.m. and 3 a.m., which is typically the time period in which most supernatural- and bedroom-based incidents occur. One night in particular, Janet was jolted awake by the sound of eerie, hair-raising laughter. Whatever "it" was, it was in the yard, "the sound drifting up through my window." Fear, and those childhood memories, which had never really left Janet, soon came cascading back in spades. And once again, something mysterious was lurking on the edge of the woods. Janet, not surprisingly, dared not to venture outside (Ibid.).

As the years progressed, the sleepless nights and the vague imagery of something tall and dark roaming the family's property continued periodically. Even when Janet moved to a city environment as an adult, the encounters and the issue of waking in the early morning for no apparent reason were yet again reignited. Of these encounters Janet told David Weatherly:

> Over the years, I've seen glimpses of him, or it. It's a very, very tall man and his arms are impossibly long. I've never seen a face, just glimpses of his head, which I can tell is bald. I've always felt as if it's just waiting for me to come outside, to see it closer and find out what it is. I think that's what it wants, but I don't think I would ever come back if I went out there (Ibid.).

"HIS ARMS WERE LONG, THEY SEEMED TOO LONG"

Also from David Weatherly is the account of Randall, who first encountered the Slenderman while he was in his early teenage years. Randall's encounter with the Slenderman, just like those of Janet and Matt and many others, occurred in a heavily wooded area. As Randall and his brother tossed a football back and forth to each other, Randall caught sight of a "weird figure" lurking in the heart of the trees. It was, Randall recalled, around "seven feet tall" and had "very long arms" that swung from side to side. For a moment, Randall felt oddly "entranced," something that echoes so many other Slenderman-themed cases in which the creature has the clear ability to affect and manipulate the human mind. Notably, Randall's brother was unable to see the thing that had so terrified Randall. For days afterward, Randall "caught glimpses" of the Slenderman, always in the vicinity of the family home (Ibid.).

In the following year, Randall and his brother went away to summer camp. It should have been a fun time for the brothers. Well, it was for a while, except for when the Slenderman intruded on the scene. It was just as the sun was going down on one particular night that the nightmare of the previous year came back to haunt Randall: Standing in the shadows of the trees was the Slenderman. *He* was back. On this occasion, however, the figure was much closer, something which ensured that Randall was able to get a better look at it. He told David Weatherly:

> The figure looked like a man at least seven or eight feet tall. His arms were long, they seemed too long; it wasn't natural how far he could reach with

them. He was wearing a black suit and his face was very pale. I couldn't see any of his features enough to describe him. I ran back to the cabin as quick as I could (Ibid.).

Interestingly, of the many friends that Randall made at the camp, one of them was a German boy, who, along with his family, had recently moved to the United States. When Randall told the boy of his experience, he suggested that what Randall saw was very similar to a German boogey-man known as "Der Schwarzer Mann," which was said to have been a "shadowy man who lurked around waiting to steal children."

Notably, the German people have a long tradition of such menacing characters in their midst. They include the Popelmann, who kidnaps kids and takes them to his marshy abode in the woods; typically, they are never seen again. Very interestingly, the Popelmann is noted for his faceless face. The Busbeller is a very similar German entity, and it is wise to avoid at all costs. As is the Bösermann, a dangerous figure in black who terrorizes children at night (of course). When else?

Of his extensive research into the world of the Slender-man, David Weatherly is inclined to go down the same path as so many others who have dared to look into the matter of the controversies surrounding the Slenderman. He says: "It may be that the collective consciousness of numerous people, spread far and wide, has co-created something quite disturbing. A modern Tulpa feeding off the fear and dread created in the stories and legends being written about him" (Ibid.).

17

"THERE'S NO STRUCTURE TO THE FACE"

Kimberly Rackley is a gifted psychic who lives on the fringes of Dallas, Texas. She has had a lifetime of paranormal experiences, including encounters with what astonishingly sound like the Slenderman. I say "astonishingly" because Rackley's experiences date back decades to her teenage years. So, yet again, we have another example of someone who has encountered the Slenderman—or in Rackley's case, Slender*men*—years before Eric Knudsen created his equivalent entity. Although many might suggest that Rackley's experience falls into the category of the Men in Black, there's no doubt that the physical appearances of her visitors have always been very Slenderman-like. And let us not forget that when Eric Knudsen chose to bring the Slenderman to the Internet, he did so by deliberately adding a significant amount of MIB-themed imagery to the table. In that sense, once again we see this issue of how the Slenderman and the MIB seem to be equal parts of one single phenomenon.

In terms of her early encounters, Rackley says:

> Since I was a teenager I've always had the same dream and then, of course, I didn't know what they were. Two Men in Black would come through my bedroom window and take me away to a place that's underground. They would sit me in a chair, with this green light that comes down over the chair. If I would reach out with my arm, it would electrocute me. It would send energy up my arm. Then, I would find myself back in bed again. I had that dream since I was probably 15. This was when I was living in Florida. Then, after that, they went away. Not until I was probably, I think, 32 was when they started to come back. From being a teenager to now, this has probably happened about 15 or 16 times (Redfern-Rackley, 2017).

Now, Rackley gets to what is without doubt the most important part; at least, in terms of the Slenderman connections to her own experiences. It's time to focus on the physical appearances of her visitors in black:

> They are always in black and they are very tall—probably six-five. There's no structure to the face; no cheekbones; none. I could see where the face should be, but it would look melted, like putty. That's what their faces always remind me of: Silly Putty; white Silly Putty. There are no eyes. And you could see where there would be an outline of a nose and a mouth, but there's nothing actually there. If you put a stocking over your face—like a bank-robber—it would look *exactly* like that. That's just how they look (Ibid.).

On this same issue of the face and the skin, Rackley noted something very eye-opening, in terms of what the Slenderman might really be: "When I see them, it's like their skin is not skin. The face moves, like a vibration, like a frequency. So, it's like they appear solid, but they're not solid at all; *they're an energy*" (Ibid.).

A stockinged bank-robber with skin like Silly Putty and dressed in a black outfit; there is, perhaps, no better description for the vague, formless face of the Internet's most infamous supernatural entity.

"THEY STILL FOUND ME"

Kimberly Rackley mentioned the vast majority of her encounters with the faceless creatures in black suits occurred while she was dreaming. This instantly provokes parallels with H.P. Lovecraft's experiences back in the 1930s with the fear-inducing Night-Gaunts. They were experiences that always occurred while Lovecraft was asleep. All of this brings us to what is known as the "astral plane." Rick Richards says the Astral Plane is a realm inhabited by "…not just disembodied souls but also inhabitants of a non-human nature, such as the lower orders of the Devas or angels, and nature-spirits or elementals (good or bad) such as fairies, which are just beyond the powers of human vision" (Richards, 2017).

Rackley expands on this issue:

> When you're dreaming, everyone automatically goes to the astral plane; but most people aren't even aware of that. On the astral plane there are different levels. Some people call them different degrees: different degrees of Heaven, different degrees of Hell, and different degrees of the astral plane. Any other entities from another realm can open doors to our astral plane when we are sleeping. So, with the right frequency, you can get on the astral plane. It doesn't matter if you're a being from Heaven or Hell, they can all access the astral plane. So, I think some of

those dimensional beings have the frequency codes to access the astral plane and that's how they meet their agenda with people who are dreaming. That's how they get into my dreams—the guys in black.

Every person has what you could call an imprint. It's a frequency. Everyone has a soul imprint which identifies them specifically. So do angels. And so do demons. But, once they have your imprint, it's like an ID code. Once they have it they can find you. Anywhere. People told me that when I moved to Texas from Florida in 2016, the dark stuff would stop, because they wouldn't be able to find me. But, they *still* found me. That's really when I began realizing that the whole soul imprint thing is probably true (Redfern-Rackley, interview, 2017).

This issue may of imprints and ID codes might well explain why some of David Weatherly's sources encountered the Slenderman throughout their lives, and at widely varying locales: Because they were essentially being tracked via their soul imprint. Now, back to what happened to Rackley in 2016, when she moved from the Sunshine State to the equally sunny Lone Star State.

"I'M FREAKED OUT NOW"

One of Kimberly Rackley's most profound and chilling experiences occurred in the early hours of June 22, 2016.

She told me, in what can only be termed as a definitive state of fear only hours after the experience took place, via Facebook message:

> Had an experience last night/morning. A little drained this morning. Freaked me out. I was awoken by what seemed like thousands of voices that were excited and upset. I sometimes hear the astral plane at night but this was crazy. I need to make it stop so I lift into astral and all these entities are everywhere in agitated state.
>
> I ask what's wrong and they all circle me and then this being, *very tall and slender, in a black suit but with a long coat* [author's italics] comes straight for me. The entities circling me close in tighter. They are trying to protect me. But he pushes them away with a flick of his hand and I'm suddenly back in my body. There, in my room, was the man. He had the same non-aura energy, like MIB. He pointed at me and the place in my wrist where the previous MIBs always try to place a chip in me started burning. Then I passed out. I feel electric inside, like I'm going to jump out of my skin and I'm nauseated. Kind of frightened. I look like death.
>
> I'm freaked out now…. This one makes the ones that come in my sleep look like puppy dogs. I'm kind of nervous about channeling or going into theta today. Too close to astral. We need to find out

why! I'll see if I can psychically discover anything. I'm not going to let them intimidate me (Rackley, 2016).

Later on the same day, Rackley expanded further on this particularly nerve-jangling experience of the night before:

If you feel like death warmed over then you most definitely look like death warmed over as I discovered this morning when I ungraciously made my way to the bathroom. You would feel and look the same if you experienced the more than unnerving events I had. Yours truly is still trembling, not quite certain if it is from the panic of the frightening encounter or the electrical jolt received.

Being a medium I am not fearful of the supernatural or unearthly, but there is one thing that has filled me with terror since I was a child and that is the MIB. I've told the story of my repetitive MIB encounters before but it suffers repeating because I believe it is significant to the most recent encounter.

From the time I was eight and witnessed a glowing figure slightly similar to a grey walking down the hallway of my home, I have been subject to frequent MIB visits. These visits are always from the same two men, mostly in my dream state until I began realizing my abilities as a medium and then the visits would occur in meditation or altered states of consciousness. Never before this newest encounter has one been a physical encounter.

The two men come to me, usually appearing through my bedroom window. My normal MIB's resemble ninjas or soldiers, always in black skintight clothing or fatigue uniforms, and always with the aura of intense panic. They will point at me and say, "No, Kya, not yet." I have no idea why they call me Kya. Is it too much to hope for that they have me confused with someone else? I also have no inkling of what "not yet" signifies. They then pull up a holographic ball where they show me that I will be taken away and put in this metal room underground. The room has one single chair and surrounding me is a bluish force field. Sounds like a science-fiction movie, right? Then they point at my right wrist, and a chip appears under my skin. They vanish, leaving me always in full panic mode.

I know you are wondering about the chip. I have yet to discover its purpose but each occasion that they place the chip, I immediately remove it. Alien or dimensional implants are more common than you might imagine and can be detected when you are in the theta state. These implants have an etheric vibration, which means they can be removed ethereally as well. Lucky for me I am a Theta Facilitator.

This newest encounter was much different than the above so let me get on with the story. I was awoken around 4 a.m. to a thousand voices in my head. It is quite common for me to hear the astral plane but this was like a war going on. I know I have to stop the voices before I end up on Zany Street with men in white coats chasing me. I lift up to the astral where I find the entities in an agitated and anxious state. Curiously they are all gathered in a very close proximity to each other.

I ask what is wrong and the entities immediately circle me. I am not afraid, as I have been to the astral many times and have friends here. Suddenly, a very tall man comes from the mist. He is in a black suit and wearing a long coat. The man is whitish-gray, bald, and no facial hair; yeah, not even an eyelash. I'm filled with immediate panic because I see no aura or residual of life force energy. The same non-energy I see with the MIB. However, there was an electrical charge around him which is something I always see around the MIB of my past encounters.

The entities attempt to tighten the circle around me but the being in black swipes them away with a flick of his hand. I fall back into my body, sit up, and to my horror the being is standing in my room. He raises his arm, palm out, and I am jolted with a shot of intense energy. I pass out.

When I awaken, it all comes flooding back to me. My body feels as if I am going to jump out of my skin and I am nauseated. I realize that the astral voices may have been attempting to warn me and certainly they were trying to protect me. This indicates that whatever the MIB are, even the astral plane is aware and afraid of them.

Could it be that my recent talk with [you] on this very subject have triggered this encounter? I believe the MIB have every account of who attempts to reveal them. I'm always left with sheer panic and more questions after an encounter with the MIB. The panic I experience however, won't stop me from seeking the truth nor will it stop me from being who I am or doing what I do (Ibid.).

"It's time to come"

As for Rackley's most recent confrontation, it goes like this:

The encounter happened when I was at the Free Comic Book Day in Folsom, California, on June 12, 2017. I was staying with a friend; it was the first night I was there and I went to bed about 10:30; I was so tired. Usually, I wake up about every 45 minutes or so; it's just how I sleep. But, that night,

I slept for four hours straight, and then I just suddenly woke up, because I felt something pulling at me; something was tugging at me in the bed.

I sit up and on the right side of the bed and there are two of the men. They had that pasty skin; the Silly Putty again; the bank-robber-stocking look. And they pointed at me and said: "It's time to come." I was like: "I don't think so!" So, I went to turn around to the front of the bed, to psychically try to make them go away. To push light at them. And, the next thing I know, literally my feet were pulled out from under me. I was dragged off the bed to the door of the bedroom. Then, they were gone; it was over. I don't remember anything after that until the morning (Ibid.).

Having carefully digested the facts surrounding Kimberly Rackley's near-lifetime-long experiences, there is very little doubt—if any doubt at all—that she has encountered beings of an extremely Slenderman-like nature. Like so many other incidents with the Slenderman, Rackley's occurred in the dream state and in the astral plane. Her visitors were tall and slender—the very description and words that Rackley herself used. Their faces were significantly incomplete and putty-like. And their outfits were always black. Put all of those components together and what do you get? You *know* what you get: *Him*. Most important of all, Kimberly Rackley's encounter of 2017 shows that the Slenderman is still being seen and still creating fear and paranoia as it sees fit.

Will we *ever* be rid of it? Will Kimberly Rackley ever be rid of it (or, in her case, rid of them)?

CONCLUSIONS

There's absolutely no doubt that we would not have a Slenderman phenomenon had it not been for Eric Knudsen. In a strange fashion, he fathered the creature; though that was surely not his intent when he lit the flame. When he created the Slenderman on June 10, 2009, Knudsen probably had no idea as to where things were destined to go. Who could have foreseen what was to come? Probably no one. With hindsight, though, we should not be overly surprised that the posting to *Something Awful* of a pair of doctored photographs should have provoked such widespread interest, obsession, and even, eventually, disturbing mania. After all, Knudsen's creation was an ingenious and eerie patchwork collection of the "best" parts of some of the most menacing figures that dwell in the domain of the supernatural: Mothman, the Men in Black, the Shadow People, and the Mad Gasser of Mattoon were just a few of them. Taking inspiration from the writings of Stephen King and H.P. Lovecraft only added to the freaky flavor. Indeed, combining the MIB and tentacle-waving Cthulhu is all but guaranteed to catch peoples' attention. And, as history has shown, it did exactly that. Big time.

But what really stood out was the incredible speed with which the phenomenon of the Slenderman grew. Recall what Ian "Cat" Vincent had to say on this very issue: "The thing that really specifically grabbed me and made the story interesting enough for me to write articles is the *rapidity* of it." It was, as Vincent rightly noted, "The right monster at the right time and for the right audience." Vincent is not wrong (Redfern-Vincent, interview, 2017).

At specific times throughout history, certain things do just seem to gel: the rise of the "Beats" in the late 1940s, the birth of rock and roll, the punk-rock explosion of the 1970s, and, of course, the dawning of the Internet—the latter, without which, the Slenderman would surely never have come to life. Or, at least, his position in today's culture would certainly be radically reduced and marginalized.

So, the Slenderman came along at what turned out to be, for him, just about the most fortuitous time possible in the history of human civilization. Even before he became a supernatural entity that stepped out of the confines of the Net and into our world, the Slenderman was already influencing minds to the point where Eric Knudsen's original posting was quickly added to, elaborated on, and then went on to spawn a wealth of Slenderman-themed blogs, websites, the *Marble Hornets* series, and even a Wikipedia page on ol' Slim himself. None of this occurred in weeks or even months. *It all happened within days.*

The amazing speed with which an idea became an undeniable phenomenon almost certainly, although probably unwittingly, led to the creation of a *second* Slenderman. Eric Knudsen's fictional freak had a rival of sorts. It's a rival that, in many respects, is seen as far more significant and dangerous than the original version. I am, of course, referring to the thought-form/Tulpa version of the Slenderman, which may have been born out of Chaos Magic. If *one* was not enough to send chills through the minds and bodies of thousands, soon there were *two* of the damned things, as was made clear when, on November 6, 2009, George Noory from *Coast to Coast AM* opened up the airways to allow Slenderman witnesses to discuss their experiences with the made-up monster.

Time and again, we have seen examples of how the human mind can—and under the right, particular circumstances—

bring to life some form of entity that is purely a construct of the human mind. Yes, the likes of Alexandra David-Neel and Dion Fortune went out of their way to deliberately try and create Tulpas—and they succeeded. In doing so, though, they found to their costs that their mind-monsters were not their friends; they were hostile, mischievous, dangerous, and malevolent things.

There is, however, a big difference between what was happening with Fortune and David-Neel nearly a century ago and what is happening now in our society and culture of the early part of the 21st century. Both women *consciously* tried to create, and succeeded in creating, Tulpas. There is, however, very little evidence or testimony that suggests large-scale attempts have been made to create a real-world Slenderman. Instead, what we have today is a massive fascination for, and a belief in, the Slenderman. That collective fascination and belief, particularly in relation to its teenaged following, has led to the *inadvertent* creation of the Slenderman, rather than a *deliberate* creation.

For the Slenderman, that distinction is utterly irrelevant: He's just pleased that he *is* here, regardless of how, exactly, he got here. And now that he's here, it's pretty much a given that he has no intention of being deconstructed. That may not be the whole story of how the Slenderman has achieved a foothold in our world, though. If it's true that we are all living in a real-life equivalent of the story that is played out in 1999's *The Matrix* and its two sequels, then just about all things conceivable are possible. In a Matrix-type world, whatever is uploaded and let loose can be considered real. Why? Because reality isn't all that it appears to be. Reality is whatever the creators *want* it to be. And that just might include the Slenderman.

That's not the end of things, though.

One of the most intriguing aspects of the entire Slenderman phenomenon is the undeniable fact that even though the creature was not on anyone's radar until June 2009, there are some truly weird stories that push the barriers of belief in such things centuries prior. The Pied-Piper of Hamelin is a perfect example. Native American legends talked of the Tall Man Spirit, which has now been upgraded to Walking Sam. Also centuries ago, Germany had the Bösermann, the Popelmann, the Busbeller, and Der Schwarzermann. They too are astonishingly Slenderman-like.

Back in 1921, the remains of a still-unidentified child who became known as "Little Lord Fauntleroy" were found in a flooded, old quarry. He was pummeled to death. In 2015, the attacker was imaged by a psychic named Marie St. Claire. She described the killer as being a slender man attired in a dark suit, and who she psychically visualized walking through woods. The Slenderman parallels are there for one and all to see. And where was Little Lord Fauntleroy found? Right in the heart of

Waukesha, Wisconsin—the very site of the May 2014 stabbing of Payton Leutner.

Moving on to 1954, there was the attack in Christchurch, New Zealand's Victoria Park—an attack initiated and carried out by teenagers Juliet Hulme and Pauline Parker. Their victim was Parker's mother, Honora, who was bludgeoned to death with a house brick. How curious that an event which so closely mirrored the May 2014 attack in David's Park, Wausheka also had a Slenderman-themed angle attached to it. Namely, that tall, black-suited figure who dematerialized before a hysterical witness. Then, there was Mike Johnson's 2001 encounter with a tall, faceless Slenderman in England's Cannock Chase woods, an area that has become notorious for a series of child-killings in the latter part of the 1960s.

All of these encounters and incidents have one thing in common, regardless of their geographical location: They all occurred long *before* Eric Knudsen created the Slenderman. Is there an explanation for all this? I refer you to the words of Robin Swope, with whom I concur when he says that Eric Knudsen unknowingly picked up something that already existed—a kind of ancient archetype.

Let's all remember, too, that many of what we might call Knudsen's "entities of inspiration" were not fictional creatures. Rather, they were established things in the world of the paranormal: Mothman, the MIB, and the Shadow People, to name just three. Even when Knudsen *did* take some degree of inspiration from the domain of literary fantasy, he chose none other than H.P. Lovecraft, among others. As we have seen, Lovecraft's creations may not have been fantasy-based, after all; they just might have been *real* monsters and malignant things that invaded Lovecraft's dreams, but which also gave the impression that what was real was actually the product of a vivid and eccentric mind—when it was actually the other way around.

John Keel, author of *The Mothman Prophecies*, warned time and time again about the dangers of thinking about, and pondering on, supernatural entities. And he offered those warnings for a very good reason: Keel, to his eternal cost, had done precisely that himself. He thought about the things he really should not have been thinking about. And what happened? He had run-ins with the very things that were on his mind. Eric Knudsen may have *thought* he created the Slenderman, but as the previously discussed material shows, we can make a good argument that the Slenderman is a very old entity; one which, in an almost primordial form, got its grips into Knudsen when he was seeking and reaching for the ultimate Internet monster. Knudsen was, then, far less a creator of a monster and far more a conduit for something that had remained dormant for a while, but which relished the opportunity to be resurrected on the world's stage.

All of this brings us to the most disturbing aspects of the Slenderman phenomenon: that which concerns the terrible and varied attacks and killings of 2014, many of which have Slenderman-themed aspects attached to them.

Up until the summer of 2014, the number of people who had an awareness of the Slenderman was pretty much dictated by those who had gravitated to the likes of *Marble Hornets* and *Something Awful.* That all changed following Anissa Weier's and Morgan Geyser's violent attack on Payton Leutner at Waukesha, Wisconsin's David's Park on May 31, 2014. In no time at all, the Slenderman was big news; CNN, MSNBC, Fox News, and many more major outlets covered the story. And, they continue to cover the story when there is something new to report on, which is frequently.

After that, we had attacks on a parent in Hamilton County, Ohio; a house burned down in Pasco, Florida; and the deadly rampage of Jerad and Amanda Miller in Las Vegas, Nevada. All of these events had significant links to the growing Slenderman phenomenon, which brings us to what is undoubtedly the most controversial part of the entire Slenderman story: Were all of the perpetrators simply unhinged and dangerous and following their own agendas? Or, given that the Slenderman is now clearly afoot and out of control in our world, could a case be made that the Millers and the girls from Waukesha did what they did at the orders of the Slenderman—knowingly or not? Were they under the supernatural sway of the Tulpa version of the creature?

It's highly unlikely that any attorney would ever even think about going into a courtroom with a defense of "the Slenderman made me do it." Indeed, it would almost certainly be thrown out of the court, as might very well the attorney, too. But, does that necessarily negate the theory that the Slenderman is real? No. It just means that the courtroom is hardly the ideal place to debate the dark domains and creatures of the supernatural.

The fact is, though, that we do know the Slenderman is being seen with increasing frequency. He manipulates minds and he instills terror in his victims in the dead of night. We also know that the city of Waukesha, Wisconsin, has a long and disturbing history of encounters with tall Shadow People, as well as attacks on young children, such as "Little Lord Fauntleroy." It did not begin with Weier and Geyser. Is all of this mere coincidence? Or were the terrible events of 2014, which the media covered so extensively, the combined product of something else? Something that is non-human?

Blaming such tragic events on the actions of a supernatural entity that we cannot fully prove exists is as reckless as it is, for many, both unbelievable and inappropriate in the extreme. While it's all too easy to see evil in every corner, more often than not that evil comes from us, not from murderous monsters. Others, though, and particularly those who have encountered the faceless beast close up, might disagree with that particular point of view. Given the sheer fear that such encounters generate, it's easy to see why some might suggest that the Slenderman has indeed manipulated people to commit violent, murderous attacks. Maybe it has done exactly that.

So where does all of this leave us? Well, it very much depends on how each and every one of us interprets the data in hand: a modern-day, fictional boogeyman or a living monstrosity that has somehow escaped the confines of the Internet? That question will likely remain conclusively unanswered until, or even if, there is an unforeseen development in the controversy; a development that just might reveal the dark truth to its fullest, most terrifying degree. The only things we can we be sure of? The Slenderman is here and he's clearly not going away.

A few, final things to think about, now that you have read this book: Will the very act of digesting these pages ensure that the Slenderman will soon intrude upon *your* life? Can you now expect to have a terrifying encounter in the dead of night? Might you see him lurking in the woods of your town? Could just thinking of the creature cause a spontaneous manifestation in your own personal environment?

CONCLUSIONS

The trick to beating the Slenderman, and keeping him at bay, is *not* to think about him. The problem is, that's not the easiest thing to do. Good luck, though....

BIBLIOGRAPHY

"Alan Moore." *www.famousauthors.org/alan-moore.* 2017.

"Always Watching: A Marble Hornets Story." *www.imdb. com/title/tt2737926/.* 2015.

"Austin Osman Spare." *https://hermetic.com/spare/index.* 2017.

Badgerman. "Unidentified 'Little Lord Fauntleroy' Found Murdered In 1921." *http://infamouswisconsin.com/ unidentified-little-lord-fauntleroy-found-murdered-in-1921/.* October 6, 2015.

Baker, Phil. "Austin Osman Space: Cockney Visionary." *www.theguardian.com/artanddesign/2011/may/06/ austin-osman-spare-phil-baker.* May 6, 2011.

Ball, Philip. "We might live in a computer program, but it may not matter." *www.bbc.com/earth/ story/20160901-we-might-live-in-a-computer-pro- gram-but-it-may-not-matter*. September 5, 2016.

Bender, Albert K. *Flying Saucers and the Three Men*. N.Y.: Paperback Library, Inc., 1968.

"Beware the Slenderman." *www.hbo.com/documentaries/ beware-the- slenderman/video/promo.html*. 2017.

Birmingham, Robert A. *Indian Mounds of Wisconsin*. Madison, Wisc.: University of Wisconsin Press, 2000.

Bohr, Nick. "Slender Man stabbing victim thriving, family says." *www.wisn.com/article/slender-man-stabbing- victim-thriving-family-says/8604292*. January 16, 2017.

Brickley, Lee. "Everything You Need To Know About The Slender Man at Cannock Chase." *http://paranor- malcannock.blogspot.com/2015/01/everything-you- need-to-know-about.html*. January 26, 2015.

———. "Proof Slender Man Wasn't Created Online." *http://paranormalcannock.blogspot.com/2015/01/is- this-proof-slender-man-entity-wasnt.html*. January 30, 2015.

Brooks, Michael. "Unknown internet 2: Could the net become self-aware?" *www.newscientist.com/article/ mg20227062-100-unknown-internet-2-could-the- net-become-self-aware/*. April 22, 2009.

Browning, Robert. "The Pied Piper of Hamelin." 1842. *http://www.bartleby.com/360/6/51.html*. 2017.

Carroll, Peter J. *Liber Null & Psychonaut: An Introduction to Chaos Magic.* Newburyport, Mass. Weiser Books, 1987.

Cassady, Leah. "Slender Man Spotted in Staffordshire." *www.stokesentinel.co.uk/slender-man-spotted-staffordshire/story-25920210-detail/story.html.* January 25, 2015.

"Chaos Magic." *www.sacred-texts.com/eso/chaos/.* 2017.

Coleman, Jenny. "Shadows of the Thin Man." *Fortean Times*, issue 317, August 2014.

Coleman, Jenny and Coleman, Loren. "Slenderman Becomes Too real." *Paranoia Magazine*, issue 59, Fall 2014.

———. *Mothman and Other Curious Encounters.* N.Y.: Paraview Press, 2002.

———. *"Slender Man Mayhem & Las Vegas Killings." http://copycateffect.blogspot.com/2014/06/slenderman2.html.* June 9, 2014.

———. "The Mothman Death List." *www.lorencoleman.com/mothman_death_list.html.* August 20, 2005.

"Constantine." *www.dccomics.com/characters/constantine.* 2017.

"Constantine." *www.imdb.com/title/tt0360486/synopsis.* 2017.

"Crooked Man, The." www.*rottentomatoes.com/m/the_crooked_man/.* 2017.

Cruz, Lenika. "There Are No Easy Answers in *Beware the Slenderman*." *www.theatlantic.com/entertainment/ archive/2017/01/there-are-no-easy-answers-in-be- ware-the-slenderman/513425/.* January 23, 2017.

Curran, Dr. Bob. *A Haunted Mind*. Wayne, N.J.: New Page Books, 2012.

"Dark City (1988)." *www.rottentomatoes.com/m/dark_ city/.* 2017.

David-Neel. *Mysteries and Mystery in Tibet*. N.Y.: Univer- sity Books, 1958.

DeLong, Katie and Beverly Taylor. "Slenderman stabbing: Morgan Geyser's trial pushed back 2 weeks to al- low Anissa Weier's trial to finish." *http://fox6now. com/2017/04/13/slenderman-stabbing-morgan- geysers-trial-pushed-back-2-weeks-to-allow-anissa- weiers-trial-to-finish/.* April 13, 2017.

Dewey, Caitlin. "The complete history of 'Slender Man,' the meme that compelled two girls to stab a friend." *www.washingtonpost.com/news/the-inter- sect/wp/2014/06/03/the-complete-terrifying-history- of-slender-man-the-internet-meme-that-compelled- two-12-year-olds-to-stab-their-friend/?utm_term=. b92f853eccea.* July 27, 2016.

"Dion Fortune." *www.innerlight.org.uk/dionfortune.html.* 2017.

"Disturbing True Story of the Pied Piper of Hamelin, The." *www.ancient-origins.net/myths-legends/ disturbing-true-story-pied-piper-hamelin-001969.* August 14, 2014.

Downes, Jonathan. *The Owlman and Others*. Woolsery, U.K.: CFZ Press, 2006.

Drayton, Joanne. *The Search for Anne Perry: The Hidden Life of a Bestselling Crime Writer*. N.Y.: Arcade Publishing, 2016.

Effron, Lauren and Kelley Robinson. "Slender Man Stabbing Survivor's Parents: 'She's Meant to Do Something Special.'"*http://abcnews.go.com/US/ slender-man-stabbing-survivors-parents-describe-horrific-ordeal/story?id=25787516*. September 26, 2014.

Ellwood, Robert S. *Islands of the Dawn: The Story of Alternative Spirituality in New Zealand*. Honolulu, Hawaii: University of Hawaii Press, 1993.

Evans, Brad. "Hamilton Co. mom: Daughter's knife attack influenced by Slender Man." *www.wlwt.com/article/ hamilton-co-mom-daughter-s-knife-attack-influ-enced-by-slender-man/3543596*. June 6, 2014.

Falk, Dan. "A self-aware internet not so far-fetched." *www. smh.com.au/technology/technology-news/a-self-aware-internet-not-so-farfetched-20120920-26ah3. html*. September 24, 2012.

"Fenrir." *http://norse-mythology.org/gods-and-creatures/ giants/fenrir/*. 2017.

Fortune, Dion. *Psychic Self-Defense*. Newburyport, Mass.: Weiser Books, 2011.

Furneaux, Rupert. *Famous Criminal Cases*. London, U.K.: Wingate, 1955.

Gaudette, Emily. "Mr. CreepyPasta Explains the Problem with 'Slenderman.'" *www.inverse.com/article/31493-jeff-the-killer-slenderman-mr-creepypasta-youtube-scariest-creepypasta*. May 15, 2017.

Godfrey, Linda. *Hunting the American Werewolf*. Madison, Wisc.: Trails Books, 2006.

Graham, Peter. *So Brilliantly Clever: Parker, Hulme & the Murder That Shocked the World*. Wellington, NZ: Awa Press, 2011.

Grimm, Beca. "'Walking Sam,' An Urban Legend Like 'Slender Man,' Might Be Inciting Teen Suicides In A South Dakota Lakota Community." *www.bustle.com/articles/80864-walking-sam-a-urban-legend-like-slender-man-might-be-inciting-multiple-teen-suicides-in-a*. May 4, 2015.

Hawkins, Jaq. D. *Understanding Chaos Magic*. Taunton, U.K.: Capall Bann Publishing, 2001.

Hine, Chris. *Condensed Chaos: An Introduction to Chaos Magic*. Tempe, Ariz.: Original Falcon Press, 2010.

"How the Living Influence Hauntings." *www.coasttocoastam.com/show/2014/05/30*. May 30, 2014.

Hrodey, Matt. "In the Woods." *Milwaukee*, January 2016.

"Ian 'Cat' Vincent." *www.catvincent.com/?cat=334*. 2017.

jackdirt. "A Chaos Magic Primer." *www.excommunicate.com/a-chaos-magic-primer/#axzz4o3CLoR5P*. April 30, 2007.

Jones, Abigail. "The Girls Who Tried To Kill For Slender-man." *www.newsweek.com/2014/08/22/girls-who-tried-kill-slender-man-264218.html*. August 13, 2014.

Kaye, Randi. "Smiley face killers may be stalking college men." *www.cnn.com/2008/CRIME/05/21/smiley.face.killer/*. May 21, 2008.

Keel, John. *The Mothman Prophecies*. N.Y.: Tor, 2002.

"Kenneth Grant: Writer and occultist who championed Aleister Crowley and Austin Osman Spare." *www.independent.co.uk/news/obituaries/kenneth-grant-writer-and-occultist-who- championed-aleister-crowley-and-austin-osman-spare-2231570.html*. March 4, 2011.

Klickna, Cindy. "The Case of the Mad Gasser of Mattoon." *http://illinoistimes.com/article-70-the-case-of-the-mad-gasser-of-mattoon.html*. May 1, 2003.

Knight, Gareth. "About Dion Fortune." *www.angelfire.com/az/garethknight/aboutdf.html.2017*.

Knowles, George. "Austin Osman Spare (1886-1956)." *www.controverscial.com/Austin%20Osman%20Spare.htm*. 2017.

Krulos, Tea. *Monster Hunters*. Chicago, Ill.: Chicago Review Press Incorporated, 2015.

Kuna, Natalia. "Shadow People & Dark Beings." *www.nataliakuna.com/shadow-people--dark-beings.html*. 2017.

LadyBlackhart. "Vodyanoy (Slavic Mythology)." *www. wattpad.com/128591707-mythical-beasts-vodyanoy-slavic-mythology*. 2017.

Lennon, Allan. "Tulpas—When Thought Takes Form." *www.huffingtonpost.com/allan-lennon/tulpas-when-thought-takes_b_7852742.html*. July 23, 2016.

Levy, Paul. "Catching the Bug of Synchronicity." *www.awaken-inthedream.com/catching-the-bug-of-synchronicity/*. 2010.

Lockley, Mike. "Spooky Slender Man spotted in Cannock." *www.birminghammail.co.uk/news/midlands-news/spooky-slender-men-spotted-cannock-8505191*. January 24, 2015.

Louv, Jason. "Introduction to Chaos Magick." *http://magick.me/p/chaos-magick*. 2017.

———. "The Strange Life of Austin Osman Spare, Chaos Magician." *https://ultraculture.org/blog/2017/05/01/austin-osman-spare/*. 2017.

Lovecraft, H.P. "The Call of Cthulhu." *www.hplovecraft.com/writings/texts/fiction/cc.aspx*. August 20, 2009.

Lovitt, Bryn. "Slender Man: From Horror Meme to Inspiration for Murder." *www.rollingstone.com/culture/slender-man-from-horror-meme-to-inspiration-for-murder-w432163*. August 3, 2016.

Lund, Rob. "Matrix City: A Photographic Comparison of The Matrix and Dark City." *www.electrolund.com/2004/10/matrix-city-a-photographic-comparison-of-the-matrix-and-dark-city/*. October 4, 2004.

"Malicious Myths: The Vodyanoy." *https://inthedarkair. wordpress.com/2015/10/05/malicious-myths-the-vodyanoy.* 2017.

"Marble Hornets." *www.youtube.com/user/MarbleHornets.* 2017.

"Matrix 101." *http://thematrix101.com/.* 2017.

Matrix, The (1999). *https://www.amazon.com/Matrix-Keanu-Reeves/dp/B00000K19E.* 2017.

Matthiessen, Peter. *In the Spirit of Crazy Horse.* London, U.K.: Penguin Books, 1992.

McAteer, Oliver. "Ghostly sightings of Slender Man reported in UK town." *http://metro.co.uk/2015/01/25/ghostly-sightings-of-slender-man-reported-in-uk-town-5035922/.* January 25, 2015.

McGrath, Jim. "Conjuring Constantine"). *https://the-laughingmagician.wordpress.com/2012/08/20/conjuring-constantine/.* August 20, 2012.

Medlicott, R.W. "Paranoia of the Exalted Type in a Setting of 'Folie À Deux': A Study of Two Adolescent Homicides." *British Journal of Medical Psychology,* 1955.

Miller, Lisa. "Slender Man is Watching." *http://nymag. com/daily/intelligencer/2015/08/slender-man-stabbing.html.* August 25, 2015.

Moran, Lee. "Florida teen obsessed with Slender Man set fire to own home as mom, bother slept: cops

(VIDEO." www.*nydailynews.com/news/national/ slender-man-obsessed-fla-teen-set-fire-home-cops-article-1.1928945*. September 5, 2014.

Moskowitz, Clara. "Are We Living in a Computer Simulation?" www.*scientificamerican.com/article/are-we-living-in-a-computer-simulation/*. April 7, 2016.

Mukherjee, Ritoban. "Unveiling the Truth Behind the Cannock Chase Slenderman." *www.huffington-post.com/ritoban-mukherjee/unveling-the-truth-behind_b_6569830.html*. January 30, 2015.

Murray, Rheana. "Teen Inspired by 'Slender Man' Set House on Fire: Police." *http://abcnews.go.com/US/ teen-inspired-slender-man-set-house-fire-police/ story?id=25262814*. September 5, 2014.

"Neighbor: Gunman Dressed Up As Slenderman, Joker." *http://lasvegas.cbslocal.com/2014/06/09/neighbor-gunman-dressed-up-as-slenderman-joker/* .June 9, 2014.

Nelson, Sara C. "Slender Man Linked To Murders Of Las Vegas Police Officers." *www.huffingtonpost. co.uk/2014/06/10/slender-man-linked-murders-of-las-vegas-police_n_5477422.html*. October 6, 2014.

"New Daughter, The (2009)." Offutt, Jason. "Encounters With The Shadow People." *http://from-the-shadows. blogspot.com/2009/03/encounters-with-shadow-people.html*. March 20, 2009.

"Optic Nerve." *http://slendermanrp.wikia.com/wiki/Optic_Nerve*. 2017.

"Optic Nerve HQ." *https://slendermanhunters.wordpress. com/2012/08/31/optic-nerve-hq/*. August 31, 2012.

Orlando, Alex. "Deputies: Pasco girl who set house on fire texted mom an apology." *www.tampabay. com/news/publicsafety/missing-teen-found- unharmed-after-suspicious-home-fire-in-port- richey/2196079*. September 4, 2014.

Ortiz, Erik. "Police Fatally Shot Las Vegas Gunman Jerad Miller During Gunfight." *www.nbcnews.com/story- line/vegas-cop-killers/police-fatally-shot-las-vegas- gunman-jerad-miller-during-gunfight-n128546*. June 11, 2014.

"Pale Man (Pan's Labyrinth), The." *www.imdb.com/title/ tt0951335/. 2017. http://slendermanconnection. wikia.com/wiki/The_Pale_Man_(Pan%27s_Laby- rinth)*. 2017.

"Pan's Labyrinth (2006)." *www.imdb.com/title/tt0457430/*. 2017.

Parker-Hulme Murder Case." *http://christchurchcitylibrar- ies.com/Heritage/Digitised/ParkerHulme/*. 2017.

Parkinson, Justin. "The Origins of Slender Man." *www. bbc.com/news/magazine-27776894*. June 11, 2014.

"Pauline Parker and Juliet Hulme Documentary." *www. youtube.com/watch?v=4RGT79Mr23I*. May 26, 2016.

"Pauline Yvonne Parker." *http://murderpedia.org/ female.P/p/parker-pauline-photos.htm*. 2017.

Pearce, Matt. "Internet blamed as 'dark and wicked' influence in Wisconsin stabbing." *www.latimes.com/nation/la-na-wisconsin-stabbing-20140604-story.html.* June 3, 2014.

Peters, Lucia. "Creep Things That Seem Real But Aren't: Slender Man." *www.alloy.com/entertainment/creepy-things-that-seem-real-but-arent-slenderman/.* May 7, 2011.

"Philip Experiment, The." *www.liparanormalinvestigators.com/philip.shtml.* 2017.

"Philip Experiment, The." *www.time-loops.net/Experiment_Philip.htm.* 2013.

"Philip Experiment, The: did a 1972 scientific experiment conjure a spirit or create a real ghost? *http://altereddimensions.net/2014/the-philip-experiment-1972-toronto-scientific-experiment-conjure-spirit-ghost-poltergeist.* April 8, 2014.

"Pied Piper of Hamelin: A Medieval Mass Abduction?, The." *www.medievalists.net/2014/12/pied-piper-hamelin-medieval-mass-abduction/.* December 7, 2014.

Piehl, Kristi. "Detectives Chase 'Smiley Face' Murder Mystery." *http://abcnews.go.com/GMA/story?id=4738621.* April, 28 2008.

Poe, Edgar Allan. *A Dream Within a Dream,* 2017. *www.poetryfoundation.org/poems/52829/a-dream-within-a-dream.* 1849.

Rackley, Kimberly. Facebook message to Nick Redfern, June 22, 2016.

Red Pill Junkie. "Slenderman & the Suicide Spirit." *http://mysteriousuniverse.org/2015/07/slenderman-the-suicide-spirit/*. July 24, 2015.

Redfern, Nick. "Slenderman: The Cannock Chase Controversy." *http://mysteriousuniverse.org/2015/01/slenderman-the-cannock-chase-controversy/*. January 30, 2015.

———. *The Real Men in Black*. Wayne, N.J.: New Page Books, 2011.

Richards, Rick. "Astral Life." *www.rickrichards.com/astral/Astral11.html*. 2017.

Roberts, Andy. "The Big Grey Man of Ben Macdui and Other Mountain Panics." *Strangely Strange But Oddly Normal*. Woolsery, U.K.: CFZ Press, 2010.

Romano, Ajo. "Is an urban legend encouraging South Dakota Sioux teens to take their own lives?" *www.dailydot.com/irl/walking-sam-myth-lakota-pine-ridge-suicides/*. May 4, 2015.

Saint Claire, Marie. "Little Lord Fauntleroy Murder." *www.underworldtales.com/little-lord-fauntleroy-murder/*. November 6, 2015.

"Sandbox." *www.techopedia.com/definition/3952/sandbox-gaming*. 2017.

Sejnowski, Terrence J. "2006: What Is Your Dangerous Idea?" *www.edge.org/response-detail/11400*. 2017.

"Slender Man." *http://marblehornets.wikidot.com/slender-man*. 2017.

"The Slender Man on Coast to Coast." *www.youtube.com/watch?v=Qzti3xDlfk0'* November 14, 2009.

"Slender Man, The." *http://creepypasta.wikia.com/wiki/The_Slender_Man*. 2017.

Slenderman235. "Interview with Victor Surge, creator of Slender Man." *https://slenderman235.wordpress.com/2011/10/20/interview-with-victor-surge-creator-of-slender-man/*. October 20, 2011.

Snell, Lionel. *My Years of Magical Thinking*. Mouse That Spins, 2017.

Snyder, Chris. ""The story of 'Slender Man'—the Internet's creepiest urban legend." *www.businessinsider.com/slender-man-story-hbo-documentary-2017-1*. January 9, 2017.

Solon, Olivia. "Is our world a simulation? Why some scientists says it's more likely than not." *www.theguardian.com/technology/2016/oct/11/simulated-world-elon-musk-the-matrix*. October 11, 2016.

Steinbach, Emily. *The Tulpamancer's Toolbox*. Kindle, 2015.

Stuart, John. *UFO Warning*. Clarksburg, W.V: Saucerian Books, 1963.

Swope, Robin. *Slenderman: From Fact to Fiction*. Erie, Penn.: Open Gate Press, 2012.

"Synchronicity and Signs." *http://personaltao.com/teachings/shamanic/synchronicity-signs/*. 2017.

Takineko. "Dark City vs The Matrix." *www.retrojunk.com/article/show/214/dark-city-vs-the-matrixDark*. 2017.

BIBLIOGRAPHY

Taylor, Troy. "Mad Gassers!" *www.prairieghosts.com/gasser.html*. 2002.

Taylor, Troy. *Monsters of Illinois*. Mechanicsburg, Penn.: Stackpole Books, 2011.

"Thelema." *http://oto-usa.org/thelema/*. 2016.

"Terminator, The." *www.imdb.com/title/tt0088247/*. 2017.

Thompson, Nathan. "Creating Imaginary Friends Is The Internet's Newest Subculture." *www.vice.com/sv/article/exmqzz/tulpamancy-internet-subculture-892* September 3, 2014.

Turner, Rebecca. "The Hypnagogic State: How to Have Lucid Dreams Using Hypnagogia." *www.world-of-lucid-dreaming.com/hypnagogic-state.html*. 2017.

"2001: A Space Odyssey (1968)." *www.imdb.com/title/tt0062622/*. 2017.

Tyson, Donald. *The Dream World of H.P. Lovecraft*. Woodbury, Minn.: Llewellyn Publications, 2010.

"Victor Surge." *http://theslenderman.wikia.com/wiki/Victor_Surge*. 2017.

"Victor Surge, Slender Man Creator: 5 Facts You Need To Know." *http://heavy.com/news/2014/06/victor-surge-who-created-slender-man-eric-knudsen/*. June 3, 2014.

Vielmetti, Bruce. "Girl claimed she had to kill." *Milwaukee Journal Sentinel*, February 17, 2015.

———. "Mother protests treatment of girl charged in Slender Man stabbing." *USA Today*, June 23, 2016.

———. "Fighting for her daughter." *Milwaukee Journal Sentinel*, June 22, 2016.

———. "Killing Slenderman: Editing a Modern Myth Before it Bites." *www.dailygrail.com/Guest-Articles/2012/10/Killing-Slenderman*. October 31, 2012.

———. "Slenderman: Five Years." *www.dailygrail.com/Forteana/2014/6/Slenderman-Five-Years*. June 9, 2014.

———. "The Slenderman: Tracing the birth and evolution of a modern monster." Published in *Darklore Volume VI*, edited by Greg Taylor. Brisbane, Australia: Daily Grail Publishing, 2011.

Vitimus, Andrieh. "Chaos Magic: The Misunderstood Path." *www.llewellyn.com/journal/article/1799*. 2017.

"Waukesha Haunted Places, Houses, And Directions To The Hill." *http://mke.hillhaseyes.com/Haunted-HouseDirections/Waukesha*. 2017.

Weatherly, David. *Strange Intruders*. Dallas, TX: Leprechaun Productions, 2016.

Weatherly, David. "Tendrils of the Slenderman." *Paranoia Magazine. www.paranoiamagazine.com/shop/paranoia-59-fall-2014-pdf/*. Fall, 2014.

"Who was Waukesha's 'Little Lord Fauntleroy?'" *www.reddit.com/r/UnresolvedMysteries/comments/29qh6c/who_was_waukeshas_little_lord_fauntleroy/*. 2017.

Wisconsin Historical Society. "Odd Wisconsin: The curse of the Hille farm." *http://host.madison.com/wsj/news/local/odd-wisconsin-the-curse-of-the-hille-farm/article_922eeafc-5d20-54fe-b0a0-5f6c9b772976.html.* February 8, 2015.

Wichtel, Diana. "Anne Perry: Life after the Parker-Hulme murder." *www.noted.co.nz/archive/listener-nz-2012/anne-perry-life-after-the-parker-hulme-murder/.* August 4, 2012.

Wilkins, Harold T. *Flying Saucers on the Attack.* N.Y.: Ace Books, Inc., 1954.

Author Interviews and Correspondence

Coleman, Jenny, interview with, June 19, 2017.

Huberty, Mike, interview with, June 27, 2017.

Jornlin, Allison, interview with, June 4, 2017.

Krulos, Tea, interview with, June 5, 2017.

Phillips, Olav, interview with, July 20, 2017.

Rackley, Kimberly, interview with, July 15, 2017.

Swope, Robin, interview with, May 16, 2017.

Vincent, Ian, interview with, June 18, 2017.

ABOUT THE AUTHOR

Nick Redfern is the author of more than 40 books on UFOs, aliens, Bigfoot, lake monsters, the Abominable Snowman, and Hollywood scandals, including *Immortality of the Gods*; *Weapons of the Gods*; *Bloodline of the Gods*; *Monster Files*; *Memoirs of a Monster Hunter*; *The Real Men in Black*; *The NASA Conspiracies*; *Keep Out!*; *The Pyramids and the Pentagon*; *Contactees*; *The World's Weirdest Places*; *For Nobody's Eyes Only*; and *Close Encounters of the Fatal Kind*. He has appeared on many TV shows, including the

Travel Channel's *Mysteries of the Outdoors*; the BBC's *Out of This World*; the SyFy Channel's *Proof Positive*; the History Channel's *Monster Quest* and *America's Book of Secrets*; Science's *The Unexplained Files*; the National Geographic Channel's *Paranatural*; and MSNBC's *Countdown with Keith Olbermann*. Nick lives on the fringes of Dallas, Texas. He can be contacted at his blog: http://nickredfern-fortean.blogspot.com.